AN ANGEL

ON MY SHOULDER

A SOLDIER'S STORY

BY

DONALD HEICHEL

Tate Publishing, LLC.

Published in the United States of America
by Tate Publishing, LLC
127 East Trade Center Terrace
Mustang, OK 73064
(888) 361-9473

ISBN: 1-5988637-8-9

THIS BOOK IS DEDICATED TO THE MEMORY OF JACOB FLEISCHER AND DALE FRACKER JR., TWO OF MY HEROES. THEY GAVE THEIR LIVES ON NOVEMBER 24, 2004, AND I AM PROUD TO SAY, THOUSANDS OR MAYBE MILLIONS OF LIVES HAVE BEEN CHANGED BECAUSE OF MEN LIKE THEM.

TABLE OF CONTENT

---✦---

INTRODUCTION

This book wasn't meant to be a book at all. I merely wrote down some things in a journal as time went by in Afghanistan. During the deployment, I decided I wanted something for my children to read later in life. Just in case something was to happen to me, I wanted my wife to know my thoughts and prayers as it was happening to me. When I sent home the first journal, she read a little bit of it, and encouraged me to put some of the incidents into a manuscript.

I hope that through the true stories, a person can understand what we are going through to bring democracy to the Middle East. Freedom is not easy, nor is it free. Sacrifice including sleeplessness, fatigue, blood, sweat, and tears are an essential part of freedom. Our grandfather's and father's knew what it was to liberate a people, and unfortunately, it can't be done in one day. The part of the world we are helping is showing signs of giving in to this new kind of thinking: independence.

My prayer is that each person who opens this book will be helped to understand what someone feels when away from family, when serving unselfishly in combat, and when a soldier deals with personal loss and tragedy in the middle of an armed conflict. Everything that I have tried to detail in this book is truth, most of which were experienced by a small group of men who would die for freedom without a flinch. Some of those men did die, and they were my good friends. I will never forget them.

CHAPTER 1

✪

VOLUNTEER

September 11, 2001–I was out of the Army, and Al Qaeda had struck on American soil. It was quoted in some of the local news media that this was the worst attack since Pearl Harbor. I vowed revenge, but only under my breath. What could I possibly do from my living room? Boycott international terrorists? Give blood to the Red Cross? I wanted to do something, "I am still able and capable," I said to myself. Maybe volunteer to help out with something here at home since I was out of the Guard.

I had already been to Iraq in 1991, and didn't really want to go back. Over the last few years, I had told a number of friends and family I already served my country and it was someone else's turn. I wondered aloud whose turn it was, because the end product our armed forces were turning out were college bound soldiers with the same philosophy as I had: Find a way to pay for college, AND gain some needed physical and mental training. The military would certainly provide something valuable I could take with me into a successful civilian career.

Just two months prior to the terrorist attacks, my new wife and I had gotten robbed in Manila, Philippines. A couple blocks from the embassy is a long street in metropolitan Manila, a prime target for tourists, but I didn't know that. We had just gotten back from doing some shopping, and were returning to our honeymoon suite, when the typhoon we were in, started to pick up. So, we picked up the pace also in order to get back to safety from the weather. My wife and I slowed between the buildings, and just as we did, a car pulled up that had 'undesirables' inside. A guy leaned out the car and took her purse while the car was still moving. My passport, military ID, and money were in her purse, all gone now. Thankfully, I had left my wallet in the hotel room, which contained our credit cards, and my Indiana state driver's license. So, they really got very little from us, even though we felt like we had been more than violated. I tried to run the car down, with its yellow license plates on it, but couldn't catch up to it. Tess screamed frantically to come back to her, and so I did. Someone was watching us up in heaven, I'm sure. We could have easily been killed.

At the police station, we gave a detailed description of the car, including the license plate number. The police asked me more than once if I was sure that the plate was yellow with green lettering. "Yes, I am positive," I declared. They went on to tell us that it must have been a stolen plate, because the only ones with yellow plates were taxi cabs. So, we accepted the fact that whoever it was, they were not going to catch them.

The whole ordeal really set me back on my timeline to return to the US, because I had a flight scheduled early the next day. Ironically, the date we were robbed was July 4, 2001. (Happy Independence Day, Don!) I called the embassy from the police station to explain the ordeal, and the duty officer was rather non-informative. I was taken back by the lack of professionalism, and the discourteous way I was being treated. The LTC who was in charge at the time actually told me it was too late at night to help anyone with a problem like ours.

I wonder what would happen if we were killed? Actually, this wouldn't be the first time before 9–11 that I had an encounter like this with our tight-shipped government. I had heard about some people in South American a few years ago on a talk show that were kidnapped similar to the people the Abu Sayyaf had kidnapped in Basilan. Rather than try to help, they simply left them to rot by themselves. Who knows if they would make it out alive or not. Well, they did, and the gentleman who was captured came back to tell his story. The government quickly tried to silence him . . . too late, he told his story to several media outlets. The media however, likes to exploit political stories and parlay them into doom for the politician they are trying to exploit. I wish the media would responsibly and equitably report the stories with the same time given to the 'small' stories.

The day of September 11, I was sitting in my living room at home, and watching the television, and while looking at the horrific live picture of the second building crashing to the ground, my mind began to wonder about what happened to my wife and I in Manila. Abu Sayyaf in the Philippines could be connected to this whole event. So, why not call the phone number on the TV (linking the FBI) and give them some information? Well, I did just that. The officer who answered the phone wouldn't even take my name. I couldn't believe it. I realize they aren't going to act on every Tom, Dick, and Harry who calls in, but I had a documented event that happened to us. I also had information about people who were probably watching the same hotels, with addresses and everything. The FBI acted like I was interrupting their coffee break. The guy listened, and then ended the phone conversation with, "Yeah, whatever. We'll get back to you if we have any questions."

I had heard about Saddam's Bombmaker (Khidhir Hamza), and how it took him several attempts to escape. He told of how the CIA laughed at him when he told them about how Saddam is building nuclear weapons. The US and our intelligence gathering systems were basically withered down to watching CNN and the 6 o'clock news on how their information was received. If that isn't trying to sabotage a nation, I don't know what is. With 30,000 employees and a six billion dollar budget, the strongest agency in the world could not determine whether this man was truly who he said he was. When they finally figured it out, months later, this man and his family no doubt would have been killed by Hussein himself had he found out. We had a horrible intelligence system, and needed to be overhauled. The events of 9–11 would be the icing on the cake.

People in America wanted answers to the string of events that followed 9–11. Especially because of the promises Al Qaeda made about continuing to strike. If they were smart, they would have kept coming at us, because from my vantage point, ALL of our defenses were down. America wanted to put the screws to this guy, Bin Laden. Immediately, if not sooner. I wanted to do something, but what? I wasn't in the National Guard anymore, and I was establishing a new career. Somebody had to stand up and help. Like grandpa Heichel said, "Years ago people did it (volunteered help), I don't understand why everybody wants to 'work' 9–5 and not do anything that means something."

In fall of 2001, I received a survey in the mail from the Army wanting to know why I had gotten out, and why I left my last unit. I was brutally honest: "I tried to get back in once, but the personnel office in Indianapolis said they had lost my records." Well, that wasn't a surprise, I had heard about the military misplacing files, and losing paperwork, and all sorts of things. Sometimes they lose paperwork on purpose, and when someone's life is in the balance, it can mean someone's career in many cases. (Funny that I put a packet in for a full-time job while over in Afghanistan, and one of the personnel officers who applied for the same position conveniently forgot to forward mine) Well, after a lot of reconstructing, and finding the "lost file" in St. Louis, MO, I started my trek back into the National Guard. My wife was still awaiting immigration procedures, and I thought it would help supplement retirement when we decide to.

While my life has been inspired by people like Zig

Ziglar, and other great speakers of my time, I have taken a lot of things for granted in life. Shortly before I deployed to Afghanistan in 2004, my grandmother, Lucille Tyskie, died at age 75. (That age is still in debate by a couple members of the family) "Grandma Tyskie will live until she is 100," I thought. She was the last of my grandparents to pass away, and as I came back from the mobilization station to attend the funeral, a lot of thoughts pressed my conscience. I have no more grandparents, and now I know that mom and dad will be next probably. That's how it's supposed to work, right? In the American Dream, everyone lives until they reach the age of mortality, then the extra years are a bonus, right? I think maybe my grandmother had something to do with keeping me alert, advertent, and alive. She NEVER said a bad word about anybody. I mean that, NEVER. I heard her complain about things at times, but it was always something a typical mother, or grandmother would worry about. She only tried to protect her family, and the life she lived. I can't say she is the angel who has been guarding me, but maybe she has something to do with it.

Grandma was so proud of her grandchildren, and great grand children. She used to give us money and candy, like any good grandma would do. Not the kind of candy kids eat today though. She would make homemade cookies and candy that we loved. I will miss that.

Before I left for the deployment to Afghanistan, my dad had told me that grandpa Heichel had a badge that he earned when he was in WWII. I told dad I wanted to take it with me so I could keep my grandparents in my mind while I was overseas. The irony is, I was awarded the same Combat Infantryman's Badge that he was awarded in the South Pacific when I qualified for it. It made me proud that my grandfather served and dad served in the Navy Reserve during the Vietnam War, and now I have been a part of Panama, Iraq, and now Afghanistan.

Dad worked various jobs in Laporte, Indiana, my hometown, at a factory. He is rather zealous about religion, and likes to share his thoughts with many different people. He loves people, and wants to share the love of Christ with them. That is something else I have taken for granted at times. Dad has never had 'great words of wisdom,' but he always said, "Do your best at everything you do." I took those words to heart, nearly always.

Susan E. Parsons (Tyskie) is my mom. Mom and I are almost exactly alike. My stubbornness, obstinacy, and utter independence are attributed to her. She says I have "Tyskie blood" in me. She's right too. Mom never was the affectionate, huggy, 'touchy feely' type of mother. She loved with the expectation that we would wise-up, or the belt would help coach us into it. It worked, too. I think I have the neighborhood record for the most whippings in one summer. To tell you the truth, I love my mom more because of it. If it were not for her discipline, I would no doubt have gotten into drugs, or worse. Some of the other neighborhood kids who were "spared the rod" DID wind up in jail, and worse. I guess I could have turned out a lot worse, who knows?

Childhood for me was short. I played everyday, as hard as I could, and then when I got into high school, I played harder. Sports and athletics taught me a lot of things, mostly about training ahead of time. I can't remember one person who never practiced baseball or football drills, doing very well. Jim Menne was my defensive back coach. I doubt I left any impressions on him, but I always tried my best, and he expected us to. If we didn't, he reminded us with "M" drills. The guys who practiced, and made something of their training, were the ones who excelled. I only wish I had applied that knowledge to my academics in high school. I was always told I could do better, but only applied it in sports. When I had to pay for it in college though, it meant a lot more to me.

In 1989, Donald A. Heichel II enlisted with 2 buddies

in the US Army. I decided to become a military policeman, and further a law enforcement career after training and duty was complete. I had watched the movie "Stripes" and thought basic training would be a piece of cake. In some ways, it was. I loved the physical training, but the mental training was really the best exercise for me. It was a challenge because your mind was working all the time, and telling your body to stop. The physical part really wasn't that much of a challenge though, I was coming off a summer of playing softball and more summer baseball. Plus, I worked a job to earn a little extra cash, so it really wasn't that difficult to do the physical training. Mentally though, it challenged me.

Well, in 1991, the Gulf War hit, and the nation was locked on the Middle East, especially Iraq. My ex-wife and I talked to her parents about us getting married before I left. They said, "Don't do it." It was like a dare to us I think. It's like they put a box of freshly baked chocolate chip cookies on the table, and told two 3-year-old kids to not eat any. We got married anyway, without their blessing.

Her father Bill was one of the nicest men I had ever met. He ended up passing away sometime in 1999, and I was saddened. It seemed unfair that someone like him would leave this world early, and in a lot of ways, it was. I knew Bill was a good father, and husband, something I wanted to be like. The truth was, I was too young to handle marriage, but I am happy Daniel and Jonathan were a product of that decision. They are two of the best kids I have known. I know a lot of people say that about their kids, but I think they turned out just the way Jennifer (ex-wife) and I wanted them to. They are very smart, analytical, and like to use their minds for good things.

Jump to 2002: After passing the security clearances, and getting through the physical examinations, I was ready to re-enter the military as a National Guardsman. There is no contract for officers, and I had completed my degree and was ready for promotion. I didn't have to come back, because my original contract was complete. The truth is I can get out when I want to now. I wish angels did paperwork . . . if they did, I would have been promoted 2 years earlier to Captain.

I told my wife late in 2003 that there was no chance a company commander would be activated for duty. "They just won't take a commander out of his position to go on any deployment, unless the whole unit was called up," I said. I was wrong. In April 2004, I was told that my duty orders were transferring me into a special position as an embedded trainer with the Afghanistan National Army. I was going to be teaching, training, and mentoring a bunch of brand new troops to fight a real enemy. The task was not insurmountable, but with Tess only here a year and a half, this wasn't in our 5-year plan.

May 23, 2004, I left for Camp Atterbury, Indiana for mobilization, and training for the Middle East.

CHAPTER 2

✪

DEALING WITH DEPLOYMENT

My wife and I were married in the Philippines in June 2001. We actually had a large wedding, compared to some of the wedding arrangements I had been to in the United States. The flowers, and large dinner alone would have cost in the thousands, but the cost of living in the Philippines is much less than it is in the United States, and it was a good call by her. She and her mother coordinated everything, and it was immaculate. I was more than impressed, and quite happy.

We met on a Christian dating service on the internet, and to tell the whole truth, I was very leery and suspicious of acquainting myself with someone who was a foreigner. Especially from the Philippines. I had heard of 'mail order' brides, and wanted no part of it. Well, after telling her in no uncertain terms, I thought she was too far away, we kept corresponding. After several months, I decided to meet her, and then it just clicked and we were married shortly after.

Now, it's no secret that immigration to the United States was no easy task. In fact, the state department had made my efforts literally impossible to achieve without the help from a Senator and Congressman. It was ultimately Senator Evan Bayh who saw to it that the process was expedited. Seventeen months is hardly what I would call expedited, but he did make it happen. The process costs hundreds of dollars, and then there are several steps to getting someone from another country over here. I couldn't understand why there were two ways to get someone to the US? One way, a person pays a couple hundred dollars, and they are guaranteed an answer within six months. The other way, a person can pay $1000 and be guaranteed an answer in two weeks. Now, I have a master's degree in Business Administration, and an undergraduate degree in Business Management, but something isn't adding up. Why would the government, who tries to make things 'all equal,' set up a system that actively promotes class warfare? I mean, if all men are created equal, why are our legislators making laws that make it unfair for honorable, law abiding citizens? I still haven't received an answer from the Congressman in northern Indiana about Tess' immigration. They must have 'misplaced the file.'

Anyway, the deployment started with a vacation. We took a two week vacation to Nevada as soon as I got the word I would be going on active duty for annual training in May, and then on a short term order to prepare for Title X orders. Our trip out west was just what we needed. We relaxed as we drove through the plains of Nebraska, the mountains of Wyoming, and the Salt plains of Utah. Nevada was equally peaceful and it gave me some time to think about all of our plans for the future, which were rapidly changing. As we drove I thought about family and friends, and how my life would be on hold for a year. Tess and I would laugh, and tell each other we will miss each other sorely.

The irony is that in 2002, when she arrived in the United States, we had been separated for 17 months, and now it was going to be for another 15 or so months. So, I made one anniversary, and even that was spent at home. Now, I would miss our 3rd and 4th due to the military. I owe Tess a huge vacation when I get back, and of course, without her support, I probably would have died in some of the things that happened while I was in Afghanistan.

The Army says it supports families, and in a lot of ways it does. But, when it comes right down to where the rubber meets the road, it's the families that take care of each other. The Army has a Family Readiness Group, but it's ultimately run by the families. Really the Army just says, "Sure, we feel family is important," but in the end, the Army doesn't contribute much to the cause other than saying they support the groups that get together. At least, in Indiana, the Family Readiness has some wonderful people running the show, and that makes it very important. They DO a lot of things; they don't just talk about it. Bobbie Krynicki is one of the best people (her husband was deployed with me) the state could ask to run the program. If she says she'll call someone, she does it precisely at the time she says. If she says she'll be somewhere, she does not fail on the meeting time. I hear positive comments about her all the time. The admirable part of that is that she rarely gets complimented or recognized as much as she should be. I couldn't thank her enough for her efforts. Tess called on her a couple times, and the answer was always prompt, professional, and always with care. Ironically, you put a good person in place, and someone tries to take it away . . . they asked her to leave while I was deployed. She got the last laugh though; she's working on the national level now.

We said what I thought would be our last good bye's the week before the first of August. Then, grandma Tyskie passed away, and COL Smith expedited a pass for me to go home to be with family. I was happy I could come home to visit with family and friends, but the circumstances were not exactly ideal. I handled it well given the fact I was about to embark on a mission where I could end up in heaven with grandma in a few short days if things started to sour in Afghanistan. (Little did I know, I was going into a 1200 year old Taliban stronghold, probably the most dangerous spot in Afghanistan - in about 15 days.) It would take guardian angels, and a whole lot of trusting people whom I never met to keep me from joining her.

Deployment into a third world country is about the

same everywhere. Since I had already been to Panama, Iraq, and the Philippines, Afghanistan had that same third world smell to it: sewage and burning diesel. The same smell was everywhere, except for Mazir-e-Sharif. That was the cleanest part of the country. But, for the most part, the people didn't use hygiene as one of their most important rituals in the morning, and it wasn't on their list of priorities. We would often see someone bathing (with their clothes on) near a stream or a river that was so brown and discolored, I often wondered why there wasn't more disease here. Then, we learned that the life expectancy for most Afghanis is somewhere around age 47. Go figure. With all the sand and dust blowing around, and the careless sanitation systems they have, it's a wonder more US troops didn't come down with serious illnesses.

They warned us ahead of time via a satellite phone: "You will get sick, we promise." Of course, I did. If it wasn't the food, it was the same dust that's been whipping around this place for the last umpteen thousand years. I first got sick at our own firebase in Deh Rawood. It was probably the food I ate with the Afghanis that got me sick, and of course I lost weight. When I got sick, I still had a job to do, and I wasn't going to let a minor illness keep me from my duties. I didn't really tell my wife, I just let the medics take care of me with whatever they would prescribe. Cipro became part of my diet about every 5–6 days, and it killed whatever I had digested. Over the course of the next several months, I would get sick on and off, usually a spout of diarrhea. Nothing major, but I wasn't taking any chances, so I visited the medic when I thought I was coming down with something. I never missed a day of work though. That's what is so amazing. With all the sickness and other things going around, I never got bedridden-sick.

As I said goodbye to everyone and boarded flight 822 to Germany, I reflected on my time at the funeral, and back home. I would miss politics, especially locally. I love my home of Laporte. I hope someday I will get a chance to help see Laporte grow and prosper and see my kids grow up to make a difference there. I thought about what awaited me over in this new foreign land. Mostly, I thought about my wonderful wife, Tess. We had spent most of the first 4 years of marriage away from each other. We needed time alone, and to be together.

Flight 822 left for Germany on August 7, 2004 at 1830 hours.

CHAPTER 3

THE AFGHAN ARMY

I would have to change command, and clear my inventory of equipment before leaving. I had just taken command the previous summer, and I loved it. The best job in the United States Army is company commander. I wouldn't trade that job for anything. I poured my soul and life into being a commander. I loved my men, and tried to lobby and protect every one no matter what the circumstances, even the guys who sometimes gave our leaders grief. I didn't care, they were **MY MEN**. Nobody messes with my men, not even the ones who were just 'meeting the standard.' When I left, I left without saying goodbye. There's no way I could have stood there and watched another officer take the unit I was helping to build. I never was a big person for long good-byes. I would rather go into the worst scenario without telling my wife or kids. It would break my heart to take a chance on leaving, knowing they didn't want me to go.

Some of the guys had volunteered themselves to come with me, but their roles would be limited to being a security detail for the task force. The job would be tedious, and one that wouldn't win any admiration from the world, but the men who got a chance did their best. I was proud of every one of them. I think there were times when they felt like their work wasn't being appreciated, but I was proud of them. Every time I would see one of them, I felt drained, but then I would try to smile and let them know I was thinking about them, and wanted to give them some encouragement. I was heartbroken that I couldn't be one of the company commanders while I was there, and that my role was doing the real fighting with foreign soldiers in the Kandahar area (Deh Rawood). I wanted to be able to lead my own unit of US personnel, but instead I had to settle for these foreign fighters that were underequipped, 70% illiterate, and barely dependable. (Crossing my fingers)

The first group of ANA soldiers (Afghan National Army) I was helping to 'train' was already deployed down-range and conducting operations with the 3rd group, Special Forces, and a couple trainers already embedded. The scenario was that we were to be combat advisors because there was little training due to the high amount of missions being conducted. So, we used the time we could to see what they had already learned, assess what we needed to work on, and then refine what they needed to brush up on. Sounds easy enough, right? Sure, but our task force really wasn't aware of the missions ETT's were being subjected to.

During one operation, a few ETT's were put into a very tight situation in Shindand. The Special Forces soldiers assigned to the area left them to hang out to dry, and the ETT's had to hunker down with their ANA forces for 2 days before they were able to move. Just a couple hundred meters away was the warlord and his men waiting to blow up anyone who was coming his way. To make a long story short, the SF guys were all rewarded with bronze stars, and the ETT's Bronze Stars were downgraded to ARCOM's. The worst part was that our men had to stand there and see all the SF guys get pinned for medals that they earned because they put their tails between their legs, and our men stayed. So much for the 'elite' hard core SF.

I'm in a foreign land, with a company of soldiers that are very diverse ethnically. There are literally 3 different ethnic groups among the 108 soldiers, and that means 3 different languages. (Dari, Farsi, and Pashto) Not dialects either; three different languages. There were times during back briefs and after action reviews that I would literally have the interpreter explain the same thing three different times. Since most of the guys were illiterate, I had to draw sand tables, and then basically have the interpreter talk to the men like they were 5 years old. (In many cases, they acted like they were 5 years old.) From smoking hashish during duty hours, to shaking down local vendors for money because they were poor, some of the men didn't understand that this was not the way humanity was designed to act. Yet, in the hundreds of years prior, its how much of Afghanistan operated. To this day, there are still these same, warlord-like mentalities. The men would need a lot of work, and Mike and I were determined to change them.

I had a lot of work to do with the ANA. We got to the point where I was telling the company commander that we needed ethics training for the leadership and the soldiers who didn't understand it was wrong to steal, lie, and cheat. I thought it was a crime to steal in an Islamic country. Apparently, the rules don't apply if the person they are stealing from is from a different tribe. Well, I was from the Freedom tribe, and I had enough of it. So, the American NCO who was assigned with me, Mike Guzik, helped along to coach the NCO's, and I the officers. We taught them how to keep the troops busy, how to utilize time to their fullest advantage, and that despite what tribe a person was from, the men needed to be treated equally. That meant from praise to punishment, all persons needed the same treatment. It worked, especially when we were watching. When the men saw others getting rewarded with certificates because of a job well done, they really shaped up when we came around. It was like the little boy who wanted to impress his father by showing how good he did, and it was working.

One time during an operation on a dismounted night patrol, we came to a checkpoint we called "Martyr Hill." I could see through my night vision the commander swinging his fists from about 100 meters away. I was near the middle of the observation post, and I went to investigate. Apparently, the troop hadn't moved to the position the commander instructed or at least not fast enough, so he proceeded to dish out his own form of discipline. Now, there are some things a US person should not do, and that is subvert another man's authority. So, I let him continue that for a while. Little did he know I was planning an officer development specifically for him that would help phase out that sort of behavior. The Afghani people had a culture that would need refining, and for them, refining means to use the power of the fist sometimes, instead of paper. Most of the leadership couldn't read or write anyway, so it would be a useless tool to give a soldier a counseling statement. He's liable to use it as toilet paper later (Which I saw one soldier do with a map sheet). I coached and mentored at an easy pace that was working. It's not something that changes overnight, especially with the habits that had formed with this commander.

Although I didn't agree with pounding on soldiers to get his point across, it seemed to work with the commander, so I let him use this for a while until I found the right time (The officer development) to explain that there are other ways to encourage a soldier to do the right thing. One thing the Afghanis love is certificates. They will take a certificate over a drink of water. They are very proud, and love to be recognized for their efforts when it is warranted. I slowly worked in a policy with the commander where he would let the NCO's discipline the soldiers. After all, it works in our military, why shouldn't it work in theirs? We also were able to teach the ANA how to task organize, using a system of arraying forces by platoon. Soon after we started rehearsals and doing battle drills, we found the NCO's working the missions more and more. On the day prior to our first mission, we were conducting a rehearsal, and the platoon sergeant whose name was Juma Khan, actually told a soldier to low crawl. I asked the interpreter to ask him why he was doing that. The terp said, "He wasn't moving to the right position, and too slow." I was very proud, because I knew 1SG Guzik was teaching his NCO's the right way to discipline, and that a soldier WILL become more effective if they are given progressive punishment, rather than the explosive type of micromanagement from the officers. Now I understood that I was working with the perfect US counterpart, and our time here would be good together. (It's true too; Mike Guzik is one of the most competent NCO's I have ever met. I believe it was working with him that probably saved my life on at least 2 occasions.)

That first group of men had been trained by Marines, Special Forces, and now a second set of embedded trainers. So, their skills were very basic, but they didn't have the advanced skills that could retain soldiers and make them want to stay. Needless to say, they would probably last about 5 minutes against an Al Qaeda operative if they were alone. We told ourselves that we wanted this group to be better than they were before we met them, and believe me, they were. But, not before sustaining a few casualties. What impressed me most about them was their skill of weaponry, and their love of Afghanistan. What we needed to help polish were their ethics in the leadership, and then the development of the NCO's. We worked extremely hard, sometimes all night long. So, between training people who were very challenging, to missing our own families, this deployment was something we were not going to waste.

Mike and I got into a good battle rhythm and eventually we would alternate giving advice, and going out on missions. One day Mike would play "good cop" and I would play "bad cop." Then we would switch off because sometimes we couldn't get things through to them without this approach. Truthfully, the fatigue would have killed us both if we had spent every waking moment together with the ANA. In our minds, we both wanted to help our ANA be better than when we found them. We had already made headway by our ethics and development programs we put into place.

The best part about Mike is that he knew what business was his, and he also knew I respected it. I think his feelings were mutual. There were a couple times we became frustrated with the ANA, but the good times and our progress far outweighed the downfalls we may have had. Our efforts were to make the best of our time. If we ever had a day when there was a little down time, we utilized our time to call home, or write home via the internet satellite connection some of the other guys had. Mike and I are a lot alike because we both saw our roles as career building for another country, and for ourselves. Our time was always spent doing something productive. Through that, we wanted to use our skills that we had learned in our years in the military for good, and to help bring Al Qaeda to justice, as well as give Afghanistan a fighting chance to survive. We both respected each other to the point that we trusted what each other could accomplish one hundred and ten percent.

I always thought the schools the army sends people to were just a 'check the block' routine that everyone attended. I heard a description of the troop transport cars in basic training that I'll never forget. Someone said it was a 'cattle car.' The irony is that soldiers in the military are still treated like cattle in many ways. You are basically coached into what your career will be like, and that when these events pass, you will go here or go there. There really is an end product: either a product of 6 years, or a product of 20 years. The only thing different than being treated like cattle is that the cattle get choices in certain circumstances. Ours wasn't a choice, but training the ANA was a part of our life now, and we weren't doing anything in a half ditched effort.

The 3rd group of guys in Deh Rawood was very accommodating, and did whatever they could to help us out, and we appreciated that very much. The two teams that were there were good from the standpoint that they wanted US success wherever they went. They didn't have the attitude, "we're Special Forces, and you suck because you aren't," well, maybe a couple. . . . They truly treated us like colleagues, because after all, we were doing what 'the tab' called for, but we didn't have 'the tab.' Whatever. I'd rather come home on a plane, ALIVE, with both arms and legs than have a stupid tab. As long as the ANA was under US control, and we were helping to support the mission at hand, they supported us with any requests. That included supporting our failed logistics system. Not failing . . . FAILED. It seemed like there was no room for improvement either. I truly believe the task force had a lot of folks that tried their best to get things done, but there were certain people that came over here because 'they were forced.' That is a dangerous combination, especially when those people are put into positions that will affect what happens to the guys downrange. The time for finding out whether or not my radio would work wasn't when Al Qaeda came-a-knocking either. I wasn't about to die because some guy in the 'rear with the gear' thought it was more important to have their batteries for their walkman while I sat at the firebase depending on a radio that needed the same batteries.

I know I gave our battalion Executive Officer and our Operations Officer (both US personnel, both great guys) an aneurism at times. I was a thorn in their side. I think my approach wasn't as tactical as I would have been if we were back in the US with no threat, but this was war, it wasn't annual training. I noticed several people during the first 4–5 months of the deployment treating it like they were on an extended AT exercise. This wasn't a joke, and if we were careless, people would die. (Ironically, 4 people were killed by an AT mine south of Kabul just a few months before redeployment, and the ETT personnel had no idea they were in the area. Maps of mined areas and intelligence reports could have been given to them before they conducted any reconnaissance in the AO.) Our mission was to deploy, train, teach, counsel, advise, fight, and redeploy with all of our assets, including (and especially) personnel. Having a successful logistics system was paramount to our mission. That's probably why I was so frustrated with the system. I think our BN staff thought I was out to blame them for the shortcomings. That was unrealistic, and showed a lack of confidence in the ability to lead. It had nothing to do with maturity, which someone questioned at one time. I had high demands, because the military isn't a democracy, it's a system that should work (and will work) if it is used properly. The truth is there were a lot of things we could get, but the people who were put in to influence those things weren't doing it. From all the company teams, to the battalion, we were all frustrated. In a couple cases, guys had given up altogether. I'm glad Mike wasn't one of those guys.

One time we requested batteries. Understand that the basic ICOM radio needs 6 batteries, and it functions on whatever frequency it is programmed to be on. Because the ANA were on a non-secure channel most of the time, they were told mission information on a need to know basis. Usually that meant withholding critical information until the last second, because of intelligence protection. After all, we didn't want any operatives in the area knowing what we were up to. (The ANA had the ability to gab on the radio about anything, and everything. Radio discipline classes would be one of our focuses during rehearsals.) When we requested the batteries though, we were expecting 1 or two cases (192 in a case) of high quality batteries. Well, we got high quality, but it was 4 little packages of 4 in each. Enough for about 6 hours or so, until the next ring supply flight 8 days later! Now that would have taken a miracle. So, we used what funds we had available to purchase batteries on the local economy. At one point, we purchased all the batteries in the village.

The task force had limited our logistic ability in a lot of ways, and it was the same way all the way to then end of the tour in July 2005. Some things could not be helped, but the ones that could, those personnel chose inaction as their first selection of leadership decisions. One time we were told there were no supplies for the ANA. Well, being the well trained, seasoned veteran of a previous deployment, I knew that was crap. So, I sent Mike back to physically look at the depot where the supplies were 'NOT.' In one instance we had requested fleece jackets for the ANA, and followed the request through the brigade.(ANA brigade) Well, on the ANA side, they basically didn't feel like going to Kabul, so that's why they were telling our battalion ETT's that there wasn't anything. The ANA were playing us like a fiddle, and the tune wasn't sounding good to me. So, when Mike arrived, he found there were over 6000 jackets. Like a replay in football, "After further review" we found all the things we requested, and recommended the ANA S4 be fired, immediately. No logistic officer in his right mind should be in a position where the materials can be gotten, if he/she would just get off their butt and get it.

Well, back to the SF, and their support. The team sergeant was very accommodating. He said take what you need, but please try to get it replaced when you can. He knew our capabilities were limited, and he also saw the last 3 ring flights (flying 7–8 days on different schedules) and that we didn't get anything on them. So, we had to deal with this impending/imploding system that was broken from the supply side. We determined to treat our men, and mentor the men the way they should be, and that was with our knowledge, our experience, and our common sense.

In January I went on leave, and just as I left, our company First Sergeant was blown up in an IED (Improvised Explosive Device). His name was Akbar, and was a soft-spoken guy with little management skills when we first met him. He was budding nicely according to Mike though, and we had high aspirations for him. In November shortly before Thanksgiving he asked me if I would take him to the United

States when I go back. The truth is I wish I could save all these people from this hole in the ground. It's a nation that is desert, coupled with poverty, corruption, and political instability all over the place. My heart broke every time I saw a shoeless child or an adult woman who had lost her husband that was begging. I wish I had a million dollars sometimes.

I have a love for the world in general, and wish I could see everyone have the kind of things we have in the US. There is so much taken for granted by Americans in the United States, I wish sometimes all Americans could go overseas just for a week or two. I told Jane, the mother of one of the boys I saw killed in DR, that people would love our nation a little bit more if they really knew how the rest of the world treated us. Folks don't realize how good they have it until they see how bad somebody else has it. When my grandfather was alive, he used to say that during WWII 'everybody just went.' There never used to be a "what's in it for me" attitude in the US, and grandpa said we were becoming spoiled rotten. I agree now. It took a while to see it, and it become apparent when I reached this deployment.

When I came back from leave, I was placed into a new battalion (kandak). Honestly, I would be lying if I said I didn't want to leave DR. I was happy to be going somewhere else, not because I didn't like the men, because I did. The reason was easy, I knew my time to leave this earth was coming, and if it were in my power, I wanted to prolong that. There were only so many IED's I could drive over, and around. There were only so many times I could participate in a Quick Reaction Force before a bullet or something would be caught by my body. So, I accepted the new assignment with the same attitude I had when I first reached Deh Rawood: "When I leave them, they will be better than I received them." The new battalion was green, and I used it as a tool to teach them things that would help them reach their potential.

I remember my stepdad calling us city slickers when

we first moved onto his farm in rural Indiana in 1984. I had seen and played with tractors, but never drove one, or knew exactly how they were used until I learned from him. Well, a city slicker was 'green' as far as a farmer was concerned. Meaning that they were unaccustomed to the farm and what it took to farm. Just like farming, infantry tactics are an art. You either know how to wield the sword, or you don't. The only way to know how is to practice, and be taught by a teacher if you want to get good at it. Our new battalion was green.

They stumbled slowly through training, and had the same attitude the other ANA had. They were willing to serve their country, but they didn't realize what sacrifice and risk was. If something bad happened, "En shah Allah." (As God will it . . .) If something good happened, "En shah Allah." That type of mentality doesn't have any business being taught in an army. Now, these new guys were as green as they come, and I wasn't taking any chances on some Al Qaeda operative pulling a fast one and pretending to be willing to join the ANA, only to shoot one of us later. So, I tested the leadership ability. The truth is that I was taken away from Mike and a seasoned group of guys, and I expected these new guys to catch on quicker and to be like the old team we had. They weren't. They were terrible, especially at the logistical aspect of the planning.

As I told myself the same thing I said when Mike and I were together: "As long as they are better than when I first got them that would be success." We were just getting the ANA acclimated to our system of training. Well, they didn't like the fact that I had a demanding tone, and even the simplest tasks they would make difficult. I couldn't see them going much further than learning the basics, because their whole attitude toward the military was, "If we do it once, we're proficient." Even in my youthful baseball days, I had to practice nearly everyday to get better. These guys seemed to be in the military to scam, scrap, and steal as long as they could get away with it, and I wasn't about to sell out to letting them do that. They would get better, but no where near the level as my last group of ANA.

It took some time, and the ANA appreciated all the effort we put forth. We even had a nice going away party at the end where I presented some of the leaders with certificates and t-shirts from my hometown of Laporte, IN. I gave them hats that read "Indiana" on them, and promoted my state and nation as best I could. The commander of the ANA actually hugged me and cried when I left. It was touching. The impact US troops are making in the Middle East is leaving an everlasting mark on their culture. Those people have seen first hand the generosity from our men . . . not the Army. Most guys like me shelled out hundreds of dollars from our own pockets to give things to that culture. Truthfully though, they don't want money, they want to be loved and respected, and that's it.

CHAPTER 4

✪

THE FIRST PATROL

We arrived in Deh Rawood on August 21, 2004. We had been in country for about a week, and taken a convoy to Kandahar, then a flight aboard a CH-47 Chinook helicopter into DR. There is only one way in, unless you want to destroy vehicle assets climbing over an impassable mountain range. Our mission was simple: Relief in Place (RIP) of the current embedded trainers, and then help them redeploy to Kabul, and then on to the United States. We spent time asking a lot of questions, and then going through about 3–4 days of learning how they interacted with the ANA. We were told how it was done, but Mike and I knew there were other leadership styles, and that ours would be a little more proactive than theirs. We liked the fact that they spared no details, and asked Mike and I several questions before we left.

We received a briefing from one of the SF commanders that there was a mission coming up, and that all 4 ETT's would be employed in the operation. The mission would consist of movement on foot to the objective, breaching a compound of suspected bad guys, and then securing whatever weapons they had, along with putting people under our control (PUC). My mind immediately went to work on what kind of rehearsals we would help conduct, and which men would be depended on for this operation. I didn't have a clue what we were dealing with, but I had an idea where we needed to be. We needed a lot of practice, and the abandoned compound next to the firebase would be an adequate training facility.

Our rehearsals began a couple days before, and while the seasoned ETT's ran the first part of the rehearsals, we just stayed behind the scenes to monitor how they were facilitating the training. During the first training activity, a helicopter landed just outside the firebase. On the helicopter was the staff of their battalion, and some of the new ETT staff. They had come to pick up our guys a couple days early (without warning of course). They had no time to pack, and so we helped them get their gear and loaded it on the Blackhawk. I was not impressed with the lack of planning, and had a short temper when it came to tardiness or missing a start time. The irony was that this was only the first of many times we would see people not communicate, or outright withhold information for their own personal gain. It seemed to be a common theme during the deployment, and one that gives me thoughts about our retention problems in the military. It's strange how taking care of your men will always solve those problems. But we always seem to have somebody in charge who wants to do things 'their way.' We are literally shooting at our own feet.

Well, Mike and I were then thrown into this without warning, and without whatever plans they had in their heads, and we were let alone to do our own planning. So, we came up with a quick off-the-cuff plan to rehearse and go over a few tasks that we thought would be practical and needful, and that would help save their life if they came into close quarters combat with any bad guys. We knew there were plenty of them in the area, and weren't taking any chances. The last thing I wanted was for an ANA soldier to die on my watch. Through the grace of God, not one ANA soldier perished in any of the stories I will tell in this book. One died of an illness, and one to an IED, but both happened after I left.

OUR REHEARSALS WOULD CONSIST OF:

*Executing a counter ambush drill
*Moving out of the kill zone
*Engage and detain per ROE (Rules of engagement)
*Maintain 360 degree security
*Secure the site
*Care for wounded, MEDEVAC (Medical Evacuation)
*Secure suspected evidence
*Cordon and Search
*EPW Operations

The ANA practiced their hearts out, and we were proud. They applied all the knowledge we had given them, and it looked like the patrol would go without any problems. There were a few details we needed to work on, but they weren't cause for alarm. They were particularly good at their pre-combat inspections and checks. They took only what they needed for the mission, and nothing else. That was impressive to me. Using only the personnel we rehearsed with, we told the ANA they needed to rest up because we were moving out at 0030 (12:30 AM).

At 11:45 PM, Mike and I got up and checked our equipment and radios to make sure everything we had was functional. Our night vision was in good shape, and body armor was on with extra ammunition. We also each brought assault packs with our combat lifesaver bags inside in case we needed them. Our weapons were squeaky clean, and we each carried 2 UBL's with us. With about 60 pounds of equipment and water, we moved up to the ANA.

We were impressed. They were ready far ahead of schedule, and it made us happy. The company commander was giving all the orders, and also saying he was leading the patrol. What?!!??! He hadn't even rehearsed with them, but was taking over the operation. Now, keep in mind that

I hadn't started the officer development program with him yet, and task organization wasn't his strong point. After all, they were using the stupid soviet model of leadership where the officers have all the answers, and the enlisted are treated like doo-doo. ALL the enlisted. Well, with his warlord background, he was calling the shots, end of story. I explained to him through an interpreter that the ANA were going to be under our OPCON for this mission because the SF and the 25th ID were going to be in on it too. He agreed to be a bystander, and watch us handle the ANA, so he did. With reluctance, the commander did exactly as I told him, and I think he respected me for telling him to back off.

In the back of my mind, I was thinking, well since the SF are planning and leading this patrol, we'll just kind of hang around and see what they want us to do. Well, the plan was for the SF to lead us up to the release point, which was about 150 meters from the compound. We would hunker down and perform a passage of lines and then the ANA were being tasked to breach the compound. Well, I had never been in a joint operation before, and I asked the team Captain where the other SF team would be. He said, "Are you taking your night vision?" I said, "Yes." He explained that I needed to lead the ANA to the RP and then I would see where the other guys were. Their job was going to surround the compound and shoot at anything that came running out. We had suspected, and known Al Qaeda elements in the compound, and they weren't letting anybody have a chance at getting the word out that we were in town, and we were not going to playing nice.

So, at about 1:00 AM, we moved out. The objective was approximately a 1600 meter hike from the firebase, and we were going to be relying on one of the SF guys to lead us to the release point. No problem. As we were walking through creeks, streams, trees, corn fields, and other vegetation, I began to think. "What if I screw this up?" Here I am a captain and an infantryman. I have had plenty of training over the years, but now I was actually doing it. What if I screw up, or my men screw up? These SF guys will not have any trust in me, nor will the 25th ID guys. This could be a long deployment if I don't do it right. After 16 years in the military, I was wondering in my mind about all the land navigation classes, and the patrolling classes I had ever had. Will it pay off from all those tests, practical exercises and ad hoc missions?

At Officer Candidate School in Wisconsin, we had a 2-week training phase toward the end where we would do nothing but tactics and infantry type operations. Those classes were designed to put us into a scenario where we learn patrols, priority of work, and basic leadership skills. Then at the end of all those classes and practical exercises, we would be 'shooting' at each other with our blanks and lasers, and then one side would say, "Ha ha, we win." Well, this was no winning situation. We were either going to kill people, or be killed ourselves. There was no observer/controller standing by with the 'god-gun' to shoot you if you messed up. If you mess up here, its asta la vista. There was no TAC officer there to scream at the top of his lungs, "You idiot!" I vaguely remember a lot of them saying things like, "what happens when you get into a real battle and you don't apply these skills?" All kinds of resistant messages would flash through my mind: "Yeah, but this ain't combat you jerk." "Whatever, we're not in combat." Well, now I was in combat, and it was real, not a game.

This was my first combat patrol. During Desert Shield/ Storm I was a military policeman. I had a basic job that meant searching prisoners, and sitting in a tower guarding the same prisoners. Pretty basic and non-combative environment. I was an enlisted soldier back then, and hadn't had any leadership training. I didn't know what leaders had to really go through in an environment like this. I knew there would be long days, but not 72 hour days, or 96 hour days. This was a basic mission though, and my duties were to deploy with my ANA, breach the objective, search it, then seize anything that looked like evidence, including persons. During the first Gulf War, I didn't have to do any patrolling, just watching, waiting, and then more watching and waiting.

Well, on the patrol, we came to the release point, and then ANA took up a defensive posture. Since I was the point man, I had to linkup with the SF counterpart by making my way along the tree line to the east of the compound, and then the SF soldier would direct me to the correct door we would breach through. Well, as I made my way down the treeline to enter the field adjacent to the compound, I could see Mike and his squad moving forward. Well, during the time we moved out, apparently one of the ANA had not been paying attention, and he thought there was a break in the formation. Well, he was right, but it was directed for him to wait there until I gave the signal to Mike with my Infrared flashlight mounted to my M4. Well, they panicked, and Mike moved out ahead of me across the field. I was thinking, "Well Mike, if it's your time, now will probably be it." We met up at the linkup point without compromising ourselves, luckily.

When we met up, we were directed to a small green door, about 5 foot high and 3 feet wide. I could see through my night vision the 4th of July going on all around the compound. There were snipers that had already been sitting there waiting for us to show, and they were signaling their positions with their Surefire Infrared Flashlights, and other nice toys the SF get to play with. But, under the night vision, only those of us wearing it could see them. The ANA had no clue how many guys were surrounding us. I didn't either until I saw all the IR glowing through my PVS-7's. There was no way the ANA were going to break the lock off it with their bare hands. The compound walls were about 9–10 feet high, and there were no windows. There was a small tower to the south east of the compound, and then another door to the north east. We chose this smaller door because this was what our informant gave us as the best spot to breach. We wanted to minimize our chance of casualties, while at the same time maximizing our chances to catch bad guys, and the weapons they were no doubt saving for us. It was extremely dark outside, and I could see the ANA and their faces through my night vision that they were scared. Who wouldn't be? There was a good chance we might be walking right into an ambush. Especially with all the racket and exposure across the field. If we were walking into an ambush, I was going first, because I was in front. At some point though, when we gave the signal, the platoon sergeant kicked in the door, and he went in first. I was a little shocked, but went in as fast as I could with the men.

Once we entered the compound, there were about 4–5 women, and 10 or so children sleeping outside on a large circular shaped bed. It looked like something out of an old British movie, and reminded me of "Knights of the Round-table." It didn't look like a bed at all, and the kids were terrified. The women were also. We had just broken into their home after all, and were about to shoot and kill anyone who stopped us. Well, they didn't stop us, they were actually halfway accommodating. When we asked them to move, they moved. When we asked them to get up against the wall, they did. It looked as though they were shocked and didn't expect us to show up in the middle of the night. I heard from some other SF guys that the Taliban usually wait for high amounts of illumination at night to fight. They also need their beauty sleep, and fighting in the middle of the night was an inconvenience for them. Oh well, doom had come, and they weren't ready, too bad for you Mr. Taliban.

We systematically searched each room with our ANA personnel, and found three men on the backside of the compound. One looked like he was about eighteen, the other two in their forties. Once we got them altogether and talked about who they were and what they were doing, we heard shots from the north part of the compound. Some guy came from around the building with an AK-47 in his hand, and the SF guys fired warning shots in his general direction. Well, since he knew he was outnumbered by several snipers in the trees and fields, he quickly, and wisely, put the weapon down. We questioned the men for about an hour, and they kept saying that there was nothing there, and they were only farmers trying to make a living. The team captain from the SF was pulling his hair out at this point, and he wouldn't take 'nobody here' for an answer. He was frustrated because we hadn't found anything. I'm sure thoughts of choking the informant were going through his head at the time.

So, we looked around a little while, and kept pondering why the informant had given us bad information. Something didn't seem right. The team sergeant from one of the teams crawled up into the tower that we spotted when we first got in there, and he found a guy sleeping with a loaded RPG (rocket-propelled grenade) launcher near him. Then the guys we had questioned changed their whole story and said that it was not their compound, and they were just staying there for the night. They told us it belonged to another guy who was friends with the local governor. That was crap. We were hopping around with ants in our pants now; we knew there was something there. But where?

Another search with a metal detector turned up a truck load of weapons buried in boxes in the garden of the compound. These guys were bad, and we wanted to give them some time to think, IN JAIL. There were numerous RPG rounds, a couple recoilless rifles, a sniper rifle, some shot gun shells (typically used to prime a mortar round). There were mortar fuses, AK-47 rounds, and other items of terrorist-type resources. The team captain said, "I knew it." We all felt the same way. They were feeding us a lot of information about nothing, and then all of a sudden, BAM! We hit the jugular.

When we took the men away, the women and children cried. I don't blame them, they were about to see their spouses taken into custody for stupidity. They know we are there to help ALL the people. I felt sorry because I heard them weep, but that's just it. They shouldn't have to cry about this. They don't have any education system, and the ones who ARE educated guard the knowledge for themselves. They think that knowledge is bad in the wrong hands, because they might just find out that grass IS greener on the other side. I think the only thing that will save this country is the education system, and the little kids who will profit and benefit from it. In the long run, Afghanistan is much better off with people who know things, verses people who know how to manipulate things, and create a population of people who blow up themselves and other people for no reason.

Some of my guys that are over here (US soldiers) have stated they want to see action, combat, that whole thing. I don't blame them for wanting to be a hero. Many heroes have come and found life too short because they thought it would be cool to be a hero. I think it's admirable that all of our troops are over here. Believe me, this patrol was scary. Not because there were any bullets flying, but because bullets COULD have been flying. It could have been a bad combination for us if they had been waiting. There was little cover and concealment, and they had enough firepower to give us all permanent headaches. I'm happy we all came out of it alive, and no one was hurt. I was equally happy that we found the weapons and the prisoners who would give our forces vital information later.

That RPG was intended for us, I'm sure. I don't know what made that man in the tower go to sleep, and I can't explain why our patrol was never attacked or ambushed. I still can't get over the fact that things went so well under the circumstances that evening. I have never seen God. I have never seen an angel. But, whatever it is that protected me that night was there. I believe in my heart it was God, maybe sending an angel down to guard me and my men. Maybe not. Maybe it was luck. I doubt it. If it was, then all the rest of the things you are about to read–the odds must be in the trillions.

CHAPTER 5

✦

THE FIRST FIREFIGHT

Well, about 10 days or so had passed, and we were preparing for a five day mission to Owbeh. The company commander, CPT Raqib, went to Kandahar to meet with his battalion commander about some pay issues and also checking on some winter clothing and sleeping gear for the men. We had a few US personnel come in at this time to support the mission we were about to leave on, and so there were a few more ANA soldiers here with them for a few days. Well, on the first night the US personnel showed up, we had trouble down at Taliban Bridge.

Our men had been tasked with a force protection mission around the bridge, and run checkpoints around the bridge. This bridge was incomplete, but it was the only crossing over the Tarin Kowt River, so we would use this spot to question passersby, and civilians in the area about Taliban movement. Although it was unfinished, it was without a doubt a key piece of terrain. This bridge was also one of the firebase target reference points, and would be utilized to run certain operations away from the firebase. There were approximately 30 ANA tasked to support the mission. In my mind, this was more than an adequate amount. We figured 6 check points equals 12 men, then 6 men in reserve, with the other 12 being a QRF (quick reaction force). That way, they could rotate personnel every 4–6 hours, and give some men a chance to rest. This was a perfect number to teach the commander and platoon leaders how to correctly manage the men utilizing task organization as the learning tool. They would learn the 1/3–2/3 rule when it came to sleeping, feeding, and patrols, and it would give them a chance to rotate back to the firebase and let another platoon have their shot at running missions from there independently. It was perfect for Mike and I, because then we could assess their abilities when they weren't being watched by us 24/7.

Since this bridge was 5000 meters or so from the firebase, we could only support the bridge in case of an attack, by our own QRF from the firebase. We couldn't call indirect fire because there were too many homes near there, and any place the rounds would hit would be danger close to our men, and civilians. There were plenty of cornfields around the bridge, giving the enemy a tactical advantage to snipe our men if they wanted to, and also they could hide a lot of crew served weapons (machine guns) if they wanted to. The vegetation was high too, so we were REALLY at a disadvantage.

We had heard some of the TTP's (Tactical Training Points) by intelligence sources in the chain of command that the enemy were trying to lure us out of the firebase, and then laying mines and other IED's along the roadsides when we left. The way they would do it is just fire a few shots, and then hopefully it would draw us out. We were cognizant that this might happen, so to reduce casualties on routine patrols, we would vary our routes during the patrol. For example, if one truck was going on the main road (whatever that is, this place had no main roads, they're all bad) then 2 others would take a lessor improved road, or a different route. We could keep each other in line of sight easily because the desert had little cover from concealing our vision.

One QRF mission shortly before this particular firefight, we had a rocket attack on the firebase. Rounds were hitting from a launch point about 4000 meters away and landing within 200 meters or so near the perimeter, and we went outside to investigate. Well, I was wearing sandals, shorts, and a T-shirt, and the SF team CPT said, "Don, do you want to go?" I said, "Yeah." He was already in the hummer on his way out, and said, "Here, take my weapon." Some guys from back home who were over here had joked about people going out on a patrol wearing nothing but a pistol belt and flip flops. Well, with an MP5 in my hand, and a chicken plate to protect my torso, there I was in that creative scenario with: flip flops, T-shirt and shorts! If the command could have seen me, they probably would have taken my flip flops and smacked me over the head. But, darn it, I was here to fight a war. I was here to fight terrorism. I wasn't going to crawl down in a hole because some guy back in the Pentagon with every hair perfectly set in place with starched BDU's protecting his career by forcing his subordinate leaders to write everything down in triplicate and then wait for a month or two before they decide to give us the green light. I was commissioned because I could make decisions, and that meant decisions where there wasn't time to get my comb out to brush my hair while 'Mohammad Akbar the terrorist' wanted a piece of me. I'm not the guy they want to go after either, because I'll come right back at you. Probably one of my many flaws: Type A personality.

Did the people in the twin towers have time to check what wardrobe they were in while their lives were in imminent danger? No, they ran for their lives, hoping to escape with just that. Did Todd Beamer have time to sneak back to the lavatory to check his hair and make sure he was in his best outfit before he tried overpowering the idiots who were plunging him to his death? I had no time to go all the way back to my hooch, (and in the mean time tell the enemy to stop launching rockets at us like I was calling a 20 second timeout) get my whole uniform on, and then deploy while Al Qaeda gets away with a chance to come back and reign bad juju on us. Forget it; I made a command decision to go, no matter what. If we need to stop and check to see what our hair looks like while our men are being attacked, our priority of work is backwards. Men's lives are more important than what I'm wearing to save them. If that means fighting in my flip flops for one quick response, so be it. I know there are people who are conventional warriors who get all their knowledge from the War College, and then they think the stamp of approval is there to let them put policies in place to make the rest of us squirm. Well, there's one policy I'll tell you about, and that's staying alive. My wife, family, and over 5,000,000 Indiana Hoosiers will back me on it, too. That's my policy, and I'm sticking to it.

So keeping in mind the fact that Al Qaeda was planning IED attacks on US personnel in our AO by sucking us out, we got our ANA together to see what the ruckus was at the bridge. The bridge was under attack according to my interpreter, John. He said they hadn't sustained any casualties, and there was a high probability the ANA there would run out of ammunition soon. The QRF would be in 4 Ford Rangers, and the SF would also accompany us. We were under the impression that the SF team that had been conducting missions with us would be our accompanying team. Well, it wasn't. It was the other team that had the best of times working out and playing Xbox for most of the time I had seen. I know they are all great guys, but I was worried about their inexperience with us, and Mike and I were already very familiar with the area because of the many mounted and dismounted patrols we had conducted. We could have (and probably should have) handled the situation ourselves. But, I wasn't making the calls, one of the other Captains was. I didn't want to step on his toes, so we relinquished our throne to them for one mission. Mike called me 'the diplomat' once. I thought it was ironic, because I tried to get along with everyone. I sought out counsel and advice if I wasn't familiar with something, and at times I even asked Mike for his input. After all, he was a seasoned veteran himself, having gone to Grenada in 1983 with the 82nd Airborne Division.

The team that was technically in charge of the fire-base did a great job of keeping things operational, and they sustained an environment that produced success for us. On this particular night though, the company commander of their teams was there, and they wanted to impress him. To make it look like they were in total command and control, they rode along. Well, we hadn't worked with them, and after 10 minutes of waiting for them to get in their gear, we radioed them and said we were moving out to martyr hill, which was a good overwatch place for us. When we arrived, there were tracer rounds, literally coming across the front of our Ford Rangers and the trucks we were in. Rounds were flying all over the place. I had heard a lot of strange things come out of people's mouths in stressful situations, but it was the first time I heard a foreigner using 4 letter ENGLISH profanity. Our terp was cursing like a sailor on his worst day. We had to maneuver first before we fired. The main reason was so our positions would not be compromised. We held our fire until we were able to array the forces we had. Then when the timing was right, we would pinch the enemy and make them either stop, or die.

We got into position, and the ANA commander was actually taking a squad by himself to the top of martyr hill (what irony that is) to use the position as overwatch. Well, we could see that the men at the bridge were firing at something in the area of the west side of the martyr hill, so it only made sense that an ANA element take up that position. When they did that, we drew fire from a corn field to the east side of the bridge. We didn't know it, but we accidentally broke the enemy into 2 forces because of the area we decided to dismount, and both elements were trying to escape. Had I known it sooner, we would have pursued them and used them like the shooting gallery at the county fair. None of them wanted the fate that surely awaited them, even if Allah was waiting with their 100 virgins, and endless supply of food and wine. So, now the ANA commander was firing at an Al Qaeda element trying to flee to the west, and we were firing at the retreating element to the east. It was easy, CPT Raqib would handle the pursuit from his side, and we would handle the pursuit to our side. So, just as we were about to move out to the corn field area, the SF team shows up.

The team CPT ordered one of the .50 cal weapons to fire on martyr hill. When Mike heard that, he said, "You freaking idiot! Those are my men!" The team CPT said, "OK, I didn't know, take it easy." The crisis was averted, for the moment. Well, none of the SF guys asked what was going on, and when they saw tracers coming from the bridge, they assumed it was the enemy firing from there. Well, if a person can visualize it, the men at the bridge were ours, and they were firing to the east and west, not at us. You guessed it; they were firing at our men. With the loud crack of the .50 cal going off all around, I ordered them to stop firing, and that those were our men. My ears were ringing and I had a huge headache from the rounds going off. They finally stopped after about 200–300 rounds, and realized they were firing at our men on the bridge. So now the guys we were attempting to stop were escaping, and there wasn't anything we could do. So, the SF team CPT and myself came up with a plan to search the fields, and move toward the bridge, and then back to the firebase to debrief. We found one old guy in a field, but he looked like he was 200 years old. They took him into custody anyway, and of course he didn't talk at all.

I was relieved because the fighting had stopped, but was taken back at the danger that we all were placed in. The guys we depended on to help actually got mad when we had things under control. It was amazing. I was angry mostly because they were trying to showboat themselves into this and make it look like they were the ones who did the work. Well, it worked, because 3 of them got bronze stars for it. For shooting at MY MEN! When bronze stars were submitted for me and Mike (in the same exact format), our BDE S1 said they were incorrect and needed changed to the right format. Whatever. I wasn't in this for chest candy anyway, I just hated the fact that those guys got the awards for shooting at our men, and then some paper pusher wouldn't process ours because he was too lazy to help out. They get administrative Bronze Stars; we got satisfaction that our men were alive, and ready to fight another day. Fine with me, I could care less about the stupid awards. (Later I would be awarded with a bronze star with a "V" for valor.)

I never could understand why the guys in the rear with the gear all got the awards, and then men who did the real fighting were the ones who suffered. No wonder our retention is so bad in the military. It's that kind of crap that makes me want to vomit. The sad fact is, the "Yes" men get promotions and awards, and the fighting men get to take it on the chin. That's the truth, too. We could fix all this by going back to a system of performance, rather than a system of "Who you know." All I wanted at this point was to get back home to my beautiful wife and wonderful family, and tell them I love them. That's all that really mattered to me after all I had been through in this war.

Later on during the deployment, a bunch of people would get upset because they couldn't be awarded the CIB (Combat Infantryman's Badge) because they were not 11B qualified. Well, after seeing some REAL infantrymen die in IED's and get shot up while most of the crying, whining award seekers sat in the rear, they can have mine. If I could give my bronze star or CIB back to bring back the infantrymen that died, I would. No doubt there are people who are here that want to further their career and get their awards in the easiest way. CIB's were ultimately blanketed to the task force, and that's all fine. But, to sit there and complain about what we get and don't get is horrible. Why is this generation so concerned about what they have and don't have? We can't take any of it with us to the next life. Besides, what good does it do for someone? It doesn't give a soldier any more pay. I'll never even begin to comprehend what those men at Normandy went through. Omaha Beach was hell, and certain death for those guys, and I never heard any of the families say, "Where is his award for it?" The ones who did survive were just happy to be alive.

CHAPTER 6

✪

OWBEH

The next mission was to find a high priority Taliban figure, and take him into custody. We would also hit three or four other targets around the area. I should say that was the plan. Anyone who has been in the military very long knows that Murphy often accompanies personnel on their mission. What can go wrong usually does go wrong. We plan and war game and figure out what our best scenario is for success, and it always looks good on paper. The final product often comes out looking different.

We moved out of the firebase at about midnight, and the illumination was zero on this night. Under a decent amount of illumination we can drive relatively easy with night vision on, but then there's the dust and rocks, and holes, and ridges, and riverbeds, and cliffs, and an assortment of other things that we don't usually plan for.

About 5 kilometers away from the firebase was Rollercoaster Hill, our first obstacle. The infantry were part of our accompanying element, and then the main effort was the special forces. They did most of the planning; the rest of us would support, and fill the roles of doing most of the work. As we hurdled Rollercoaster Hill, we came to an area we had to navigate at a 90 degree angle, and didn't realize there was a drop off on the north part of the road, which we were traveling from east to west. Well, one of the infantry Hummer's fell into the embankment, and they tried to drive out of the hole instead of getting recovered by one of the larger trucks with a wench on it. So, the transmission fried right there. We were one hour into a 5 day mission, and already we were down one vehicle. Murphy had been riding in our back seats.

About an hour or so later, another Hummer showed up, and we were able to continue with our movement north. The dust was terrible, and I was leading the ANA element right behind the infantry. Well, their driver had conveniently left his blackout drive lights off, and I was starting to lose my patience, as well as the tracks of where they were. The dust was so bad I could not see anything in front of me with or without the night vision on. At one point, I had to travel outside the road just to see the dust from the convoy. I was sure that on at least two occasions, I lost the convoy. Well, I knew the area fairly well, so I knew I was heading in the right direction.

Mike and I were traveling separately though, because we believed in having our ANA counterparts with us at all times. They couldn't get mentored if we didn't talk with them, so he kept the First Sergeant with him, and I kept the Commander with me. We each were assigned an interpreter, so it was easy to task organize into separate elements. The guys performed rather well without any of the neat toys we had with us. They had no map reading skills, no night vision, no global positioning systems (GPS), no communication with air assets; we were their lifeline, and they knew it. If anyone messed with our ANA, we were there to protect them.

We traveled about 15 kilometers or so north to the north fording point on the Helmand River. The river was deep enough that a Ford Ranger or Hilux could navigate through it without flooding, but we didn't want to take a chance. In order to make it across, the truck needed just a little gas, and then it would literally float to the bank, and then the truck could maneuver across on its own power. The SF had 2 ATV's with us for greater mobility off-road, and then the infantry had an LMTV and a couple Hummers. The other vehicles were GMV's the SF had.

Just before we forded the river, one of the vehicles' brakes went out. We were sure that something happened, but were so far back, we waited until one of the ATV's came back to spread the word. The commander of the convoy and his vehicle had broken down. So, there we waited for about 2 hours until it was fixed.

After all were fixed, it was about 4:30 AM local, and we could tell the sun was starting to come up. It was time for each vehicle to cross the river. Each truck slowly made their way across without a problem. I felt the ranger start to float, and then as the front tires reached the bank, I hit the gas, and the truck made it across. Mike, who was right behind me, must have panicked a little bit, because he hit the gas, and the water shot up into the engine and flooded it out. The rear vehicle, which was from the infantry as security, also flooded. Initially I thought Mike had caused the infantry Hummer to flood because he stalled, but that's not what it was. Whoever did the preventive checks and maintenance on the vehicle must have skipped the part where a soldier checks the air intake. The filter was gone! It flooded the motor immediately.

The last 2 vehicles in the convoy got flooded out, and stalled the convoy for two more hours. So much for the element of surprise. The sun was coming up higher and higher now, and if someone had any communication with the local talibs, they knew we were in the area, and where we were headed. There is only one way someone can go in the direction we were headed, and it would be easy to warn the enemy if they knew we were there. They had to have known by now.

The SF mechanic was a genius. What can I say? This guy could probably have rebuilt the entire motor in the Hummer, and the Range Rover if he wanted to. He got both motors dried out, and running again in the two hours we were stalled. During that time, Mike and I used it to make sure the men had enough water, and the NCO's were rationing proper amounts of food. The ANA would eat their whole supply in one day unless they are being watched, and we wanted this to be one of those times they didn't. We didn't need to leave a trail of MRE wrappers or empty water bottles to let Mr. Al Qaeda know where we were heading.

By 6:30 AM, we were feeling the effects of fatigue because of sleep deprivation. Dawn was quickly approaching as we headed north again over the pass. I urged our men to keep moving forward and stay close to the plan as we headed into the village we were about to raid for a bad guy. Of course, our element of surprise was gone because of all the noise we made on the other side of the pass, but we did our best.

We arrived around 8:30 AM and of course the house we raided was empty. As the ANA systematically searched the house, one of the infantry spotted someone sprinting about 250 meters away. We ordered them to halt, but he headed for the corn field on the east side of the town. He was obviously someone we spooked, and probably thought we were coming for him. It might have been the target, but doubtful. We think he was probably a scout and was going to either warn someone we were there, or he was trying to avoid capture himself. After a few hours of searching through the village, making contact with local officials, and running ourselves ragged, we decided to call the attempt on the first target off. It was time to find a spot we could hunker down in for the night before the next movement.

Just before we left, one of the interpreters from the SF collapsed. I quickly retrieved my CLS bag from my assault pack, and assisted Mike the SF Medic. We were worried about the guy who was down, and he would no doubt have to be MEDEVAC'ed out. They immediately called for air support, and set up a landing zone to get him out. He had suffered heat stroke. It was well over 100 degrees at this point in the late morning, so it wasn't a surprise. After that, Mike and I monitored each other, and also the ANA to make sure there would be no more heat casualties today. We were concerned, but confident in our abilities to help each other.

At about mid-day we moved out to the pass we had come from, and made camp for the night there. Mike and I slept on the ground, and the ANA took security on the mountain tops while the rest of the men slept. We wanted 100% security around the camp. The local police said that 3 men were murdered, execution style, in this same area by suspected taliban militants, and they probably had scouts out looking at our movements.

The next day we were up around 0200 to prepare for movement and make sure the ANA were conducting their rehearsals correctly. They are well known for 'cutting corners,' but I didn't want any of them getting killed while they were assigned to me, so we sort of micromanaged them for a couple days. After we felt comfortable, we had the men stand by.

This mission was going to be an air assault with ATV's used to run down any fleeing, suspicious people, and we were to cut off the elements in some mountains about 30 minutes or so of flying time away. Mike would take 9 soldiers, and I would take 9 soldiers on two different helicopters. Then two other teams of American soldiers would create a blocking position down in the valley to keep anyone from escaping. Then we could secure the whole village, and take our time questioning the local population about Al Qaeda and its movement.

About a week prior, there were 200 motorcycles stolen from a dealer in Herat by force. Then, there was also intelligence gathered that said there were 200 Pakistani militants training in the same valley we were about to raid. Their mission was suicide bombing anything that opposed their agenda. So, obviously we were interested in seeing to it that they could harm no one.

When we arrived though, it was like a ghost town. Well, one of the alphabet soup agencies that were along for the ride apparently sent in an observation chopper ahead of time to prepare a good landing zone for us. Nice move. The few people that were there said that everyone was on vacation. No kidding.

So, after we 'cleared' the village of 90 year olds and 9 year olds, and determined it was safe, we hunkered down outside the village for the evening. The ANA took up their defensive posture once again, and we made our way to rest.

The next day we headed back and got intelligence that there were IED's being planted along our route. The terrain was so rough, it was our only way to go through there, so we tediously moved along, and even sometimes stopped to have a mine-clearing team secure the path for us. Mine clearing literally takes hours, and even days in some cases, because it is all done by hand, and it must be done slowly to ensure there is nothing that can harm us. Well, the guys located an IED, and the SF engineer used some explosives to detonate it before we drove over it. This was just one time where I could have, and probably should have been killed. After all, we were in the lead while everyone else trailed. I hate to admit it, but I can't wait to get back to driving in Chicago where people curse at you, and don't let you in when you signal. I miss that . . . at least I know there aren't any mines or IED's waiting for me there.

CHAPTER 7

✪

THE IMPROVISED
EXPLOSIVE DEVICE

When I first got deployed, we heard a lot about IED's. The training mobilization station showed us photos of some IED's that had been found, and I had an idea that the people putting these together were ignorant of the advanced technology that exists. We were told that the taliban were idiots when it came to such technology, and to a certain extent they are. They use whatever they can to cause disruption, bring down morale, and hurt US personnel coalition forces. Little do they know that we will not back down from a skirmish if we can help it. I am very proud that our men have stood their ground like loyal soldiers should.

An IED, or Improvised Explosive Device, is basically a booby trap. It is made out of natural resources, or some ingenious manmade object. It is easy to conceal, and like most IED's they are usually buried in the ground, or put inside of trash, or some other way to camouflage it. Some IED's are relatively easy to locate, and they have some kind of explosive that is used as employment. Most are detonated by pressure plates, but the enemy has been known to use radio control to detonate them.

We trained our men to dismount at any choke point, or suspected area of IED employment, and physically walk up to the area and report any findings. We taught our men to slowly stagger a formation in case an IED were there. That way it would minimize casualties, and give our men and other vehicles opportunity to scout the area in case there was an ambush. Many times the enemy would blow something up to draw attention away, and then attack from behind, or launch some rockets or RPG rounds at us while we were securing a fighting position. At other times, they would just bury them in the road, and watch our movement. When we would get close, or if it looked like we were coming in the general direction, a battery would be attached to the initiator far enough in advance for it to blow up when we would get near the emplacement. Other times, they would lay mines under the surface of the road, because the roads were in such poor condition, and most had rocks or gravel as a base. So, it was easy to conceal something underneath the road.

On October 4, 2004, our patrol moved out north of town to scout out a possible taliban hideout. The compound was about 150 meters off the main road, so we would have to dismount the vehicles, leave guards, then move forward as quickly as possible to keep the element of surprise. It was mid morning when we arrived. So far, so good. Our men were broken up into 2 teams and sent with two government contractors that had bomb sniffing dogs to find any ordinance or illegal ammunition being safeguarded.

When we got to the compound, we questioned the people who were inside, and asked them if we could search their compound. Aren't we nice? In the middle of a war, and we're asking permission from Mr. Terrorist-hider? That's one thing that has always ticked me off about the military. Yes, we can make decisions on our own, but if it's wrong, you're on your own. That's crap. We weigh risk and take the path of least resistance in every scenario. I can't speak for the officers who don't think first before they act, but I know I weigh risk on the time I have, and if it looks bad, I don't do it. The age of attorneys basking in the cases of ridiculous and frivolous lawsuits was upon us though, so we asked first.

The guy told us, "Go ahead." When we started the

search, everything was fine. We didn't find anything, and when the intelligence personnel were questioning the man and his family, they were actually very accommodating. We didn't find anything in the compound. I didn't think we would either, this guy wasn't a talib, we could tell. He even offered to have his wife cook us dinner and have chai with him. We moved systematically just like we had in the last search. Nothing.

In the next couple compounds, we didn't find anything either. They were awfully nervous we were there, though. We could tell they were not your typical Afghani. Most Afghanis were like the last guy: cordial, inviting, pleasant, and generally good. These people smelled of badness. One of the dogs got a hit off one of the walls in a room. He tried digging through it at one point. We got a metal detector in there, and it turned up nothing. We had noticed that the talibs were getting a little smarter by moving their weapons to different locations, and even burying them inside the walls, or in the family garden, like the last guy did.

When we finished, we got outside and started back to the vehicles. On our way back, one of the SF guys who had joked about smoking marijuana was standing in a two acre field of it. The funny part about it was that there were 3 empty MRE bags sitting next to the area he entered the field at. The MRE's were from the ANA (so he says), so we concluded that he did not in fact smoke any of the man's crops. Marijuana was still legal to grow, and drug interdiction wasn't a priority at this point, so we let it go. Besides, what would happen if we had burned the guy's field? He probably would have likely used the profits to feed his family for a whole year or more. That would have made us another enemy, one that we didn't need at this point.

We left to head back to the firebase, but before we did, we were sent to scout a spot where there was a suspected anti-aircraft gun. It took us about an hour and a half to get 10 kilometers. Like I said, the roads are horrible. Even a 2.5

ton truck would not fit on some of the roads, or would be impossible to recover, so we did not bring them on most of the roads in Deh Rawood. When we got to a good overwatch position, we got a better look at the suspected weapon. It was a wheel barrow. Well, we came up empty for the day and everyone was pretty tired.

When troops get tired, they feel battle fatigue. It makes some people sleepy, some people irritable, and honestly, careless. We had been warned to not become complacent. Well, we really weren't complacent, but there are times when the hours and days pass with nothing happening. Trust me, Mr. Murphy always shows up when a person least expects him to. Well, he was ready to make an appearance.

We were coming up on a place we nicknamed "roller coaster hill." It is a sight. It literally feels like you are on a roller coaster when you drive over it. It has a very steep incline on both sides of the hill. If a large truck attempts to navigate over it, it probably will not make it. The uparmored hummers were having trouble because of the weight it carried. With the rocks and the severe grade (it's probably 45 degrees or more, literally) usually we needed a running start to get up to the top, then the smaller hills were much easier to climb. Today, I was in an uparmored humvee.

About 7 months prior, two special forces members were killed at the base of the hill. The black dust still lingers there today as a remembrance of the two men that died. I had heard that the humvee that was blown up burned for an entire day. There really was no way for them to get around it either, because there is a riverbed on one side, and then a cliff on the side of the hill itself.

As we approached the hill, we were cautious about it, but for some reason, the guys who were in the front did not have the ANA dismount and take the lead. We told them they should stop and let the ANA go first, but they didn't. Well, about two thirds of the way up the hill, there is a short dip before it climbs again. As each humvee passed, I felt safer as each truck passed. There were 4–5 humvee's and Toyota Hilux trucks that made it past the small dip, and then as the two canine guys passed with their dogs, BAMMM! The hood of their Range Rover launched into the air approximately 150 feet, then landed 60 or so yards from the vehicle. The tire, still attached to the tie rod, blew out to the right, and landed down the side of the hill. I saw hundreds of pieces of metal lying on the ground, and some of their gear. One of the men had been completely knocked out of the vehicle. This was probably a misplaced anti-tank mine, because had it been aimed closer to the undercarriage, and not the motor, both men would be dead, and their dogs.

My mind raced. I panicked a little bit, because I was 2 vehicles behind when this all happened. What if it had been me? There were only 7 vehicles in the convoy, and this one vehicle hit the IED. My chances were good that it would have been me. We had intelligence telling us that they were targeting uparmored humvees in the area because they thought it was our most expensive piece of equipment. Little do they know that our most expensive piece of equipment is human beings. The billions we spend in training, and in salary, and schools, and clothing, and family support, etc . . . little did they know. A $50,000 humvee doesn't mean anything to the army the way human lives do. As I sat there in shock for a few brief moments, I thought about my family. Every time I got shot at, every time I saw something happen to someone else, I thought of my wife. I thought of my kids. I thought of grandma Tyskie. I thought about the stupid fighting and bickering families do at home. None of the trivial things matter. Nothing mattered at that point. Two men needed help. Both former special forces members, and now government contractors, it didn't matter.

I was sure they both were dead. There was hardly anything left of the front of the truck. Both tires were gone, the hood was gone, and many of the components were completely destroyed. The first man on the scene was not me. One of the team captains took charge and already had medics helping them both. Both men were talking; that was a good sign. I knew they would need a MEDEVAC for sure. Both men would eventually walk again, both had pins put in their feet. One of the guys, sadly, went home immediately after the incident. He didn't want anything more to do with the operation, and was very vocal about not coming back. I couldn't blame him. His life almost ended, and we hadn't found anything that day. Who WOULD blame a person for not wanting to take another chance? I didn't. I appreciated the help he gave while he could. The other guy, though, he went to Germany, got fixed up, and came straight back. I was proud of them both, regardless.

Well, we would be put to task to search the neighboring compounds for any evidence or knowledge of watching anyone plant the bomb up on the hill. The ANA had found an IED in the same hole about 2 weeks prior, and we wanted to know who was putting them up there. For the night, we put a patrol out on the hill, and secured it with the local police the next day. The irony of the police taking it was that we had suspected the local police of fighting us at night, and smiling and waiving at our faces by day. It wouldn't surprise me if they were. It is common knowledge that warlords around the country were playing both sides of the fence. They each were waiting to take their turn at taking over. So if the current president lives long enough, they have a friend, and if he dies, they're friends with whoever kills enough people to take the reigns. That's the way power has passed over the last 500 years, and its not about to change.

After this IED, we were being very cautious, especially with the upcoming elections. We didn't want anymore of our men hurt, and we took everything serious. The UN would be struck by an IED a couple days later, and then 4 policemen would also be killed by a land mine. We also got reports that some taliban leaders had come from the north, in the mountains, and kidnapped, tied up, and then took 4 people up to Charcina to kill them. Then the next day they brought the bodies back and told the village that anyone caught collaborating with US people would have the same result.

The next day, we went back out east to search all the compounds from Roller Coaster Hill to Myandaw. When we got to about the third compound, we saw a guy on a motorcycle in the next compound take off like he was 5 minutes late for his morning prayer. Keep in mind it's about 6 AM now, and people are still praying and also working. It's a lot easier to work in the very early morning in Afghanistan, because of the 130 degree heat at times. Well, we chased him on foot, and the ANA continued the pursuit when they fired some warning shots for the guy to stop. Well, he didn't; he kept going. I guess if I was getting shot at, I would get out of the engagement area as soon as possible too.

So, after pursuing the guy on foot, and radioing the SF that we were far ahead of the main element at a certain grid coordinate, they told us they would linkup with us where we were at. It was all open fields for about 2,500 meters, so we could be easily seen. I waited there with 2 of my SF buddies, and we chatted while the main effort found a way to get to us.

When they arrived, we all mounted up, and took a drive to see if the guys at taliban bridge saw anything. Well, wouldn't you know it? As we were traveling along the road in our vehicles, we came across a couple guys who looked like they had just come home from hunting deer. Well, most deer hunters don't wear black, and since there are no deer here, and they had loaded AK-47's, they probably weren't local police. Well, as we got a little closer, we noticed them coming from a cornfield that is just north of the TK River. The TK River flows toward taliban bridge. We figured they were probably out either watching us, or they might be some of the guys who have been attacking taliban bridge when our men were securing it.

As we got within 150 meters or so, they took off running north. Bad move. Not with all the firepower we had with us. So, we dismounted. I told the SF I would have our ANA element secure the vehicles, and then I would be shortly behind them. There we were running through cornfields that were about 5 feet high, and running through houses chasing 4–5 taliban undesirables. About 3 minutes into the pursuit, I heard shots fired from an M4 to my right (east). One of the guys we were chasing got hit. We asked several of the villagers if they knew the guy, and they all said he was from somewhere else. He had a very clean cut beard, and was in decent clothing, with a gunshot wound in his left arm.

Mike and I had recently coordinated getting our men combat lifesaver qualified, and it's a good thing we did too. The ANA soldier, who had just completed the class, put a tourniquet on this guy's arm. Most of the SF guys wanted to put one around the guy's neck, but we were civil about it. We treated anyone we caught with dignity and respect. This guy had fired at us, and we still were able to get him proper medical treatment, miles away from any civilized hospital. Had the ANA soldier not applied it correctly, the guy would have bled to death for sure.

The rifle he had was thrown to one of his cohorts. So, all we found were a few traces of footprints, some rounds they had shot back at us, and then we had this talib in custody. The SF took custody of the guy, and the last I heard he was in Kandahar probably giving us information about where his buddies were. If he didn't, it was a long flight to Guantonamo Bay.

So, as a result of the IED the previous day, we had two men that needed medical attention and one guy we captured from the sweep of the village. The people really weren't surprised when we came knocking at their door. In fact, I think they expected it. They seemed very cooperative. They were still a little indifferent toward us, so we really couldn't trust anyone. Not even the village elders.

To this day, I believe Afghanistan still has a lot of bad guys living in it. Even some of the top government officials are playing both sides of the fence. All the 'what ifs' about Enduring Freedom must be going through their minds. Or, someone is telling the people to prepare for our departure. If we left tomorrow, this country would be right back to square one. Warlords would be scraping each others eyeballs out for the top tiered position, or there would be civil war between the warlords. I think there are still a lot of people that take bribes here. In fact, its commonplace. I only hope the people realize that our mission here is to help them get back on their feet. I believe this nation could be good, but it will take a long, long time.

CHAPTER 8

✦

ELECTION DAY

The morning of the election I was up around 3 AM to prepare for the movement west of town. We had a platoon of ANA and an SF team with us and our job was to visit 5-6 sites. I had to bring my night vision, because we would be driving in total blackout drive (like we had a dozen times before). I also had my interpreter with me and 2 ANA soldiers in an uparmored Humvee. I figured if there was an IED, at least I had armor to protect me. Little did I know that about a month and a half from now, it would change my thinking forever.

The SF guy in charge of our movement was a great guy. He would bend over backwards to get us the things we needed, and all we did was treat them with the same respect we treated every other US soldier. It was ideal for us, because we were having a lot of logistical trouble getting supplies and updates about movements, etc. Anyway, when we were back at the base camp Marty and I would joke around, and had some good discussions about politics and general state of our nation. We had a lot in common, so he was easy to talk to. I think he was realistic about what we were doing, and how much risk was necessary, all the typical officer stuff.

The ANA platoon sergeant was Jumah Khan, and he would help out with moving the ANA and task organizing everyone in case of ambush, and what each role our men would play. When we would get to a village or near a city, he would take the ANA in to meet the elders in the area, and ask how the election was coming along. Jumah was an exemplary leader. He believed in our cause, and trusted Mike and I one hundred percent. He NEVER questioned a decision we made. I truly believe if we would have asked him to go into a home alone and clear every room, knowing there were armed Al Qaeda, he would have done it. He was totally loyal to us, and that won my heart over immediately. I knew I could give him a suggestion, and he would probably take it.

There were a couple times he would be asked to make decisions for himself, and then he could make the right choice because of his experience with leading. When I was pulled out of Deh Rawood in December 2004, and then went on leave in January 2005, I found out Jumah had been hit in an IED, and the 1SG was killed. Jumah was permanently disabled, and to this day I do not know what ever became of him. He was one of the best ANA soldiers I crossed paths with.

As far as the SF goes, I always thought they were the elite of the elite. You know, the guys who you ask to complete any mission. That really isn't their role, although the men we were with would have done just that. Well, I learned a few things while I was out. The SF were ordinary soldiers, who were experts at everything they did. Everything. If they were asked to become a marksman with a certain weapon, they would practice and practice until they hit 40 out of 40 every time. Or, if they are asked to train an army for a certain nation, then they will not stop until that unit is fully trained and capable of fighting for themselves. Sometimes if they are called to do search and destroy missions, like now, they ask for whoever is supporting them to support with whatever role they ask. I was more than happy to be in this situation.

The SF were asking me and Mike to do just that: Fill in the gaps and help. Since Mike and I had worked together for the last 5–6 months, we were very trusting, and knew what was expected of us. Mike was asked to go with one team, and I with the other. The rules of the election were that no US personnel could be within 300 meters of a polling place. Fair enough. So, we had our ANA dismount, and check to make sure they weren't pulling what happens in the US at our own polling places, like stuffing ballot boxes. I never could figure out why the strongest government in the world could bring democracy to a third world (more like fourth world) nation like Afghanistan, and we couldn't even keep track of our own elections. Im still scratching my head that more than 100% of the people voted in Milwaukee. Then on top of it, we are changing to paperless voting. That will ensure that a third party NEVER gets in office. Nice way to play the game: Pick out all the aces and deal them to yourself, wish I could do that.

Anyway, we were to visit a couple schools, and a few polling stations throughout the day, and then we would come back to the firebase and help secure ballots for the UN. A few days before, there was a UN truck that struck an IED (Italian Mine) and it disabled the vehicles left front wheel. The mine was so old that most of the explosive had crystallized and was unable to produce a charge throughout the explosive. So, needless to say the UN decided it wasn't going to stay in Deh Rawood because of that IED. They were afraid of these people. I don't blame them. If someone tried to kill me, I would have felt the same way.

At one point during the day, we came to the crest of a hill and saw a truck take off in a certain direction. It was obvious they were probably scared, taliban, or just somebody driving like many Afghani's do: like they're half crazy. We didn't engage them since they were not a direct threat, but we did make note of the color and how many people were in the vehicle that way if we saw them again that day, we would have cause to stop them and question the suspicious behavior. Our mission today was just to make sure there was no disruption, and deter anyone from making a nuisance of the area.

On our way to one of the sites, the ANA had a flat tire on their Kamaz truck. In fact, two flats. The problem is, the tires are so large and bulky, the truck can carry only one spare. So, they decided to move all the weight of the soldiers to the front of the truck, and then drive it with weight on the axle that had the good tires. So, they continued the mission with no air in the back two tires. Not the best plan, but it WAS a plan in my opinion.

Like I said, I was tasked to be out west with the executive officer of the SF team, and Mike was out east closer to the 'metropolitan'(whatever that means) part of the village of Deh Rawood. We each had a platoon of ANA with us, and were to ask the ANA to just check on the poll workers and election sites to make sure everything was all right.

Today actually was a light day. My interpreter John and I talked about politics, and even had a discussion about Afghani culture and how Muslim people deal with family life and the rules of treating other people kindly. John elaborated that the Muslim people believed a lot about freedom and seeking independence for their own lives. They long for a free market and the will to do as a person pleased. He also said that the culture forbids killing of any kind, even to Christians. John and I became close friends, and I wish I could bring him to America with me. But, in the end, John really wants his country to be its own entity with the same rights as any other country. The problem Afghanistan faces is that many people are uneducated and cannot think for themselves. They often rely on someone else's opinion rather than thinking for themselves. That is probably why wrong traditions are passed down and followed blindly.

Over the course of the day there were almost no problems. The only thing that happened was that Mike and his team found an IED before it went off. It was a relief to know that everyone got back safe and that the election was a success.

Today was also Mike's birthday, so we celebrated with the ANA when we got back to the firebase. I was happy that Mike and I were still alive to be able to celebrate. I think our friendship will last for a long time after this, because of our commitment to professionalism and dedication to duty. I will never forget him after this is over.

CHAPTER 9

✪

THANKSGIVING

It took several days to put this chapter down on paper. Death isn't something people see everyday, up close. It is a life changing, extraordinary event. When I went home, I didn't talk about it to my wife. I didn't talk about it to my kids. I didn't talk about it, **PERIOD.** I was in love with the fact that life was a bowl of cherries, and I would never have to talk about some experiences I had seen. I thought, "Well, the first IED wasn't bad, nobody was killed . . . how bad could it really be if the first two guys survived?" A soldier can rationalize all day long, but the fact is, I hadn't seen someone die up close. I was invincible, like so many other people my age think they are. They're not.

I coped with death by shuffling it away in the back of my mind, and trying to make excuses and blame myself, blame others, blame anyone for it. I tried to explain to myself several times that it only happened on the news, in some other world that existed in Iraq, not Afghanistan. As of the time of this writing, 205 soldiers have perished in Afghanistan. That's roughly more than 1.4% of the total US population in Afghanistan. The truth is in Iraq, where there is ten times the amount of personnel, more people are dying per capita in Afghanistan than they are in Iraq. The numbers are disproportionate, but the media uses the larger number to manipulate their political agenda back in the US.

I remember one of the soldiers who died within our Task Force when their convoy struck a mine. They had been driving off the main road conducting a reconnaissance, so I was told. I read in an online newspaper about how the wife of one of the soldiers said, "Nobody dies in Afghanistan." Tell that to Pat Tillman. Tell that to the other 205 soldiers who have perished there. I wish I could go back in time where the rubber met the road on a political level, and made some diplomacy changes in history that would have made all this mess just go away. I'm not sure how I would do that with what President Bush called "The axis of evil." The truth is our country has always stepped up when freedom and democracy cried out for help. In my opinion, nobody who died here, died in vain. They died for a cause, whether we liked it or not. I would never want to have been president when those decisions were being made.

I think because we are reservists that had been called up, some people see us as living in some 'support role.' We're here doing a mission we were called to do, and part of that mission is to seek and destroy the elements that are trying to do harm to us. If we sat back and waited for Al Qaeda to come to us, the result would be devastating. We waited for years while Saddam Hussein sought weapons of mass destruction, including nuclear warheads (which he produced). Our role was to train these Afghanis to fight and defend for themselves. We do whatever it takes to accomplish that task, including deploying with them into situations where the risk could be critical to catastrophic. Of course when I called home I told my wife we were training most of the time.

On November 24, 2004, we moved out on a patrol to the east of the firebase, and then around to the north part of Deh Rawood to a small village called Myandaw. Our mission was to sit down with the village elders and gather information about the school situation for the civil affairs guys that were with us. We would need SECFOR, ANA, and then the CA guys to do the talking. We took one SF guy with us on the patrol, who had just arrived. They were in the process of conducting relief in place with the old teams, and then would eventually be in charge. We were more than happy to help with getting him oriented with the area for future patrols and operations in the area.

After the Pre-Combat Inspections with the ANA, I headed out in my uparmored Hummer with my interpreter and one ANA soldier. The First Sergeant that was with me had just gotten there also, because Mike was on leave, and he took a Ford Ranger with some ANA. The infantry took some guys, also, to present a heavier presence of firepower, and also help with security during the convoy. We all met outside the front gate and did our final checks on gear, ammo, MRE's and water. In the mid-morning, we left for the east side, as planned. My Hummer was in the front of the convoy. I believed firmly in leading from the front, and this time was no different. We did have one Toyota Hilux with a couple ASF guys and an interpreter, but I was the lead US vehicle.

About 150 meters or so from the start point, I felt some uneasiness in the way the hummer was running. It was a brand new vehicle that had almost no miles on it, so I was wondering why the hesitation with the engine. Seconds later, the power steering pump literally blew up. Well, now I had no power steering, and it was losing fluid quickly, so after I checked the engine and determined I needed to take a different vehicle, I headed back to the firebase. (A Humvee's power steering fluid also feeds the brakes with the same fluid, so I was running out of brakes.)

I was embarrassed. I knew the SECFOR guys were probably quietly, and in some cases openly, heckling me because I was an officer. I've often heard people say that some officers are not very competent, but I have 16 years of experience with the equipment, and knew I had the knowledge to work a large part of Army equipment. I hated when things went wrong, especially if it was partly my fault. I disliked being late, and this was no different than a bill being paid on time back home, or making sure my wife had her birthday present ON HER BIRTHDAY. We were running behind schedule now, because of my Humvee, and I wanted to get another vehicle as quickly as possible. I jumped into the last Ford Ranger the ANA had, and started out.

We got to rollercoaster hill (east checkpoint), and dismounted the ANA just like our rehearsals. They secured the hill, and when we knew it was safe to pass, we did, slowly one vehicle at a time. As we passed the north side of the hillside, we could see at the bottom of the hill how the ground was blackened from when two SF soldiers had been killed in an IED strike back in March. I often thought we should rent a local dump truck and pour sand over that area, but no one ever did. The charred remains of blackened rock and sand remain. It left a remembrance that we needed to be careful. We were, and each vehicle made it through safely. As we all passed, I'm sure the same thoughts were going through everyone else's mind: "I wonder if I'm going to blow up now?"

After the meeting with the elders in Myamdaw, we were relieved that they wanted us to help them, and return there to talk more about operations in the area. We weren't totally convinced they wanted to see us at all, but after the meeting we felt reassured that they were receptive to talking at least.

As we approached taliban bridge, we saw what was left of the ASF checkpoints that were there a couple weeks before. We had heard about the 4 local police that were killed when their vehicle hit an IED in the area we were in just the week or so before we got there, and didn't want to take any chances. In October, there was also a UN vehicle hit by an old Italian mine, but only did vehicle damage. (Ironically, the UN wouldn't even help during the elections because they KNEW there were Al Qaeda cells in the area.) So, the ANA led from the front, and as each vehicle crossed the Tarin Kowt River, we felt assured that it was safe to pass, with each one driving through the fording point after another. The river was very shallow, so it was easy for the vehicles to pass.

I passed with my ranger, then another, then another. The Humvees crossed, and just when I thought everything was safe and we were on our way 'home,' I heard a horrendous explosion. I thought someone had dropped a 500 lb. bomb on our position, and that we were being attacked. I dismounted from the vehicle immediately. There were no gun shots like I expected. Even though I was probably a good 100 meters from the fording point, I was the first one to run as fast as I could to the origin of the explosion. Usually we would not dismount like that, but there was no one attacking us, so I felt safe to evaluate the casualties.

When I came up on the scene, I saw what I most dreaded. There was an uparmored Humvee sitting about 100 meters in, literally blown in half. I carefully did a battlefield assessment, and wanted to make sure none of our men were following me into a probable minefield, or engagement area. Then I heard someone moaning. I thought for a second that if I rendered first aid on the guy, I would be the only one doing anything. So, I made a swift decision to put the men into a defensive posture. I immediately told a couple of the NCO's that were present to get the men into a 360 degree radius around the site, but watch for an ambush. We were in an extremely vulnerable position, and I didn't want anymore to go wrong than what had already happened.

I identified a combat lifesaver, and had him evaluate all the casualties. The man who was conscious needed help, and I was certain that he was going to die. The other two men were being evaluated by the troops we had, and I was doing everything I could to save time, while keeping the rest of us alive too. I called in the grid coordinate, and also prepared a red smoke grenade for identification when the MEDEVAC showed up. The driver of the vehicle and the man in the turret were killed instantly. Both men were thrown more than 60 feet from the vehicle, and had several injuries all over their bodies. We did all we could for them, but the truth is, they went painlessly into the next life.

I can't say enough about people who give their life without mental reservation. These two men are two of my heroes. They deserved more than the Bronze Stars they were posthumously awarded. They selflessly gave themselves 100 percent to whatever the task was at hand. I couldn't have asked for a better couple of men to help bring Al Qaeda to justice. My mind will always remember that day as if it were yesterday. They are a product of the resolve we have to help other peoples of ALL nations.

You see, there had been reports about Al Qaeda targeting uparmored Humvee's because of the great cost associated with manufacturing all the armor plating and the components that are expensive. So, we knew this going into the mission. That's part of the reason I took my Humvee. My truck had driven over the same hole that their Humvee had driven. I could have been the person in that explosion had the power steering pump not went out.

I stood there waiting for the MEDEVAC to show up, and thought about the whole scenario in my mind several times. I thought about how inside I was cursing and telling myself I looked like a buffoon for having my vehicle break-down, and it was my fault we were late. I thought about how I drove over the same spot, along with 4–5 other vehicles before the IED exploded. I thought about how the other infantry kid was killed in June in the same exact spot. I didn't really think that I was also a target, and probably would have been killed had the vehicle not broken down.

Then, the clouds of guilt, blame, sadness, and other hurtful feelings started to lift. I thought about my wife. I thought about Daniel and Jonathan, and Sarah, and how I would come home in January for leave to love them, and hug them. I could still tell them I love them. These two soldiers will never do that again. They can't go home to their mother and father anymore. They have become part of history that most of us dread. Nobody wants to die on purpose, let alone an accident. Maybe Jacob and Dale took my place, I don't know. I know that there is something about this incident that will never leave my thoughts. I can NEVER repay the debt I owe. These two boys are my heroes.

Do I think God sent an angel down from heaven to purposely break my Humvee? I don't know. But, it's strange to get a perfectly functioning vehicle, and then all of a sudden it breaks down. Maybe it was luck. Yeah, right. Who knows why things like this happen. I haven't had complete closure from this whole thing, but someday, I hope I will be able to tell Jacob and Dale thank you for their service, in person. Maybe in heaven.

Thanksgiving was obviously a let down. Some families would get phone calls from our men saying hello and that they can't wait to get home in a few months. Two other families will get a greeting from the military telling them their sons will not come home. I don't think my wife and family would have handled it very well. I volunteered to sit in a tower for the infantry guys so they could call home to their families and greet them. It gave me time to reminisce about the prior days events, and do some soul searching.

I called Tess and I almost couldn't talk. If people say that infantry officer's don't cry, you are mistaken. Maybe all the tough guys are so bold that they have no heart. Well, I do. Those two kids had become buddies of mine. Even though I was an officer, we had a brotherhood about us that no one will ever take away. I wasn't as close as the members of the platoon, but I had worked out with them, and had gotten to know them well enough that it felt like I lost two brothers. I had. When Tess answered the phone, she seemed like her usual caring, loving self. She always made me feel like I was cared for, even though I wasn't home. I couldn't speak clearly, and she knew something was wrong.

As I spoke to her, I told her what happened, and that there was an awful result. I wanted to jump through the phone and come home. She was concerned of course, wanting me to resign my commission, become a conscientious objector, whatever it took to get me home safe, and for good. One side of me wanted to crawl into a hole for the rest of the time I was here. I couldn't do that because of the rank, the position, and the importance to show the men that we don't quit because of adversity. We take the time we need to recover, and then we drive on. To think this is an 18 month tour was becoming a mammoth task. Even my first tour in Iraq was no where near what I was experiencing. I needed to keep my guard up though, and not become a needless casualty myself.

Where would we be if everyone just quit? What would have happened if Churchill or Roosevelt had not made the decision to drive out the Nazi's? We probably wouldn't be here today. There probably wouldn't be any Arabs or Afghanis either. If so, they'd be speaking German. Our task and purpose doesn't change, and it took a couple days for me to regroup. Thank God we have taken the proactive approach to this. Yes, there have been casualties, but no where near what would have been if we had not stepped in.

CHAPTER 10

✪

UPARMORED APPARITION

Consider this chapter a political interlude. I guess I have always been an independent thinker somewhat, so I wanted to address some issues that came up during the deployment. The politics involved in the uparmored humvee are interesting, and I wanted to address a couple things in this chapter. Hopefully my opinion of the situation won't upset too many people. Nevertheless, America needs to know how a soldier feels about it.

In December 2004, just a couple weeks after the explosion that left two of my friends dead, an Army Reservist asked Donald Rumsfield a question about uparmored humvees. He said something to the effect about why soldiers had to rummage through "rusted scrap metal and compromised ballistic glass that's already been shot up, dropped, busted, picking the best out of this scrap to put on our vehicles to take into combat." I heard there were several hundred other troops there to applaud the dissenting remarks. One would think he would at least follow the chain of command about why they were sent into harms way without the proper equipment. If it were my men going out into known hostile areas, I would not send them out without the proper amount of security. Any NCO in my command that does not conduct proper pre-combat checks WILL BE FIRED.

Now, upon analyzing the question and thinking about the times we went into combat in Afghanistan, I would agree and disagree with the soldier. Donald Rumsfeld, in my opinion, gave the best answer. "You go to war with the Army you have," he said. I believe he gave an honest, non-politically motivated answer. Guess what!? He was right. I remember going to the 1991 Gulf War, and we didn't have half the equipment today's Army has. The truth is, we had much less equipment, but were not afraid to face any foe with what we had. There is no doubt that it would give someone an appeasing feeling to know they had an uparmored humvee to drive, but truthfully, a humvee WILL NOT survive a direct hit by an anti-tank mine. I saw it first hand in Afghanistan. They don't have near the amount of mines in Iraq than there are in Afghanistan.

Some of the information provided to the press by Lt. General Steven Whitcomb was as follows:

"Up-armored humvees . . . is a vehicle that is produced in a factory back in the United States and it essentially gives you protection, both glass and on the armament on the side, front, rear, sides, top, and bottom. If you'll think of a protection in a bubble, that's the kind of what the level-one up-armored humvee gives you."

(Started using)"add-on kits that we might be able to produce that gave that vehicle additional protection. We call that level-two armor, and it's better known probably most places as add-on armor. It is factory produced, so it's built under controlled conditions, and then it's either–can be put on back in the states. But we've got 10 sites here in the theater, a couple here in Kuwait, and eight sites up in Iraq itself where we can bolt on, add this armor to existing unarmored vehicles. It gives you protection front, rear and sides, glass. It does not give protection at the top or at the bottom of the vehicle. So it gives you better than what you have with no protection on a humvee, but not quite the level-one protection."

"Of those vehicles that don't, some numbers of them are things like tool trucks, communication vans or vehicles that don't leave the base camp. In other words, they're trucked into Iraq-or in cases before what we're doing now, were driven up into Iraq-and they go onto a base camp, and that's where they spend most of their time."

"The humvee was a vehicle that was not designed to afford armor protection, nor were most of our trucks. They were designed as cargo carriers. The only up-armored humvees, the high-end ones, we had were for our military police forces. They were not for use by-as we see them used today with the number of forces."

"Add-on armoring runs anywhere from about a thousand pounds of steel plating up to about 4,000 pounds of additional weight. So a lot of our vehicles, as you point out, are not designed-their engines aren't designed to carry perhaps an additional ton of weight, the suspension and transmission."

"The other thing we've got-and I won't talk about it because it is very sensitive-is we're leveraging technology, how to detect where IED's are, who's using them, how they're being set off and those kinds of things so we could go out there early and kill those guys before they're able to execute."

Now, my opinion on these comments. What they won't tell you about the humvee is that uparmoring these vehicles is a terrible call. From the individual soldier's perspective, they really don't mind it. The upper echelon in the leadership of our military know it's a horrible call to uparmor these. It takes more time, and more money, all to appease someone. Truthfully, the kevlar that was originally installed was a perfect deterrent for small arms fire. Uparmoring these vehicles slows them down, causes more maintenance problems, and makes soldiers more vulnerable than if they were just plated with kevlar and thicker windows.

The humvee was to replace the old jeep and I think it was a good call to do just that. It was never meant to be an armored vehicle, and it never will be good for that. The reality is that our media has politicized this issue into making the current administration look stupid, and cost our taxpayers unnecessary worry and financial burden.

I remember hearing about a guy who became frustrated with the local government. He took his bulldozer and strapped on a bunch of steel, and proceeded to run down the local police station. Then he decided to take his same vehicle and run over the mayors' office. Notice that he armored his bulldozer. Why do you think he didn't use his regular car or truck? Well, common sense tells us that you don't load down your small economy car with 4,000 pounds of material to protect yourself; you will be dragging the ground and burning up the tires. He armored his bulldozer because it is meant for that much weight. The same goes for the humvee.

Now, maybe you can scream about 'sacrificing our troops' blood for Bush,' or saying, 'our troops deserve the best.' That is true, we do deserve the best. But, I am saying that maybe the argument should be to listen to the troops and not the politicians on this issue. You see, you may actually be arguing for something that is hindering your troops, not helping them. A humvee is not meant to be an armored vehicle, so what is the alternative? Give everyone a tank? I don't think that is a good solution to a long-term problem.

The biggest problems we face are that a new vehicle takes years to get into place. The media shouts, "They need it now!" That isn't possible. Usually a new project takes years to test, money to budget, and then approval from the biggest bureaucracy in the world: Congress. They will look at which Defense Contractor gave the most to their campaigns, which vendors will support them in the next election, and then of course, who will do it the way they want it (play ball).

I know of a lot of soldiers who only joined for the college money and extra income on the weekends. The truth is, there aren't many men left who joined because they wanted their families future secured. Most of those guys, who joined for selfish reasons, complained and gave leadership a very hard time because they didn't want to be there. None of us wanted to be there. Nobody prays for war. We all pray for peace right? But, when there is the duty to protect freedom, whether it is here or across the ocean, we need to go. Freedom isn't free. My grandfather and many others went to WWII thinking about that very concept. Many willing to give their lives for the sake of securing freedom and independence from those who want to force their political agenda on people. In WWII though, grandpa knew, like many thousands of other men, there was no guessing or wondering about not going. Everyone went if they were called, no complaints. Some even went who weren't called, many of them buried at Normandy.

Some people in the country have criticized the Bush administration for them 'not acknowledging the magnitude or seriousness of the dangers in Iraq,' but I disagree with that statement also. Most of those people have tried to tie that into the so-called problem with uparmored humvees, but that isn't the problem. The problem is the seizing of political opportunity for the benefit of a career, instead of the benefit of supporting the troops. Any Congressman or Congresswoman can say they are in support of the troops. But, are they voting that way? We will see. In the very next opportunity for Congress to step up and make a difference (after the Army specialists' question to Rumsfeld), they voted on allowing recruiters equal access to institutions of higher learning, and then 'Commending the Palestinian people for conducting a free and fair presidential election.' I don't understand, but why is Congress wasting its time on other countries, and not on our own? I'm not an expert on federal government functions, but being an avid political junkie, isn't the US Congress' role to be in the interests of the people of the United States, and not Palestine? Why are they wasting time on voting and debating other countries' problems, when we have problems of our own?

The problems with the uparmored High Mobility Multipurpose Wheeled Vehicle (HMMWV) are not lack of armor. The problems with the humvee are in the utilization of the equipment. To me, it's waste, fraud, and abuse to send soldiers out without consulting the intelligence officer in the battalion. This can often lead a commander to make a different choice of route, or even send out an advance party on foot to recon an area first. More than once we received information about suspected enemy and took a different route to disrupt the enemies' intention. I would never send out my men with all the equipment into a known zone without being fully prepared first. Any leader that would needs to be relieved immediately. The best thing for a company level officer to do is confirm the order with a superior, and if it is a 100 percent of contact with the enemy, recommendations on implementation should be voiced. A commander who voices concerns that are legitimate will always earn the respect of his superiors.

Truthfully, a good commander wouldn't just tell his troops to work 9-5 and then drive around Iraq or Afghanistan like they are out cruising around on a Sunday afternoon along Lake Michigan. They ought to be continuing with dismounted patrols, using the Iraqi police to help with conducting patrols, and launching stakeouts of suspected enemy areas such as the road leading into the Baghdad airport. Why are we not continuing with setting up night observation posts, and keeping our troops occupied with work? The number one reason troops get disgruntled with their leadership is not that they miss their families. Heck, we all missed our families. The number one reason boils down to boredom. When a soldier is given time to stew and become depressed, they are battle fatigued. A US soldier is the finest piece of equipment the Army has, why we don't care for it and encourage it more than we do, I will never know. (Not me though, more than once I pulled tower duty and gate guard to help my men understand I cared for them.)

Now that the media has successfully exploited the question posed to Donald Rumsfeld, we've had the chance to appease the crowd that wants to put billions of dollars into it. I disagree with throwing money at it. Every other government program that costs billions of dollars has failed miserably. Money is not the answer to the problems we face with the humvee. Look at the 'War on Drugs.' We threw billions on that, and more kids are using drugs today than ever before. We threw billions to help the airline industry, and they still lose your luggage, make you late, and treat you the same way.

The problem is with quality of leaders. It doesn't matter who the soldier is, leadership should be able to get the most out of a soldier. I know of several leaders who were given bronze stars because of their service. I'm sure they earned it, but how many of them were in actual combat? I would venture to guess that none of them faced a 40 minute firefight like Mike and I did. I would say none of them had the opportunity to drive over an IED on at LEAST one occasion. (Good thing it didn't go off or my wife would have had to write this from my journal.) I wonder how many of those guys actually saw people die, and had to call in a MEDEVAC to save someone else? I'm not saying I'm a hero, but at least my bronze star was totally justified. (By the way, it was upgraded with a "V" device by the theatre commander, and I received it in July 2005)

Our Army is craving for leadership. We need some people who will provide a good example of decision making so that our soldiers won't ask questions about equipment and what they do and don't have.

CHAPTER 11

✪

HELICOPTER SLINGLOAD AND ANA BATTLE HANDOVER

Mike had gone back to Kabul for leave, and now I was with another team member. The BN Sergeant Major was tasked to cover down for Mike while he was going home to visit his wife and 6 kids. So, we were preparing to move all of our things back to Kandahar, and then prepare for training another kandak or company. Whatever the leadership would decide would be fine with me. I was ready to leave after the latest incident anyway. I had 4 months of firefights, IED's, rocket attacks, and general life-ending scenarios I needed a break from. Besides, I would be going on leave myself in about 5 weeks, so I was all for sending me back to get settled down a little bit.

On December 1, 2004, we were preparing to leave Deh Rawood. We had been told the French would be relieving us, and they would take over our area of operation. What a joke that was. The French basically said, "Huh? You mean you want us to go on missions?" They said they would not. Go figure. No wonder they are in the state they are in. There are times I think we should have let the Germans roll in and take it all over. Then they'd all be speaking German.

I remember when France wanted us to sit back like little appeasement minded cowards during the Rwandan problems in the 1990's. Under the old administration, we did just that, and over 800,000 people perished because we sat back and watched. 3,000 UN peacekeepers were sent. I think they must have stayed in hotel rooms playing XBOX all day, because people died and a tyrannical maniac took over. Nice move Mr. France. Good thing our current administration has the cohunes to say "Enough is enough."

One day at one of our battle update briefs one of the staff officers made light of the French weaseling out like little whining cowards. He said, "Raise one hand if you like the French. Raise both hands if you ARE French." I had to laugh. They would rather put their tail in between their legs and let the tail wag the dog I guess. I'm not really sure what they are doing here in the first place. Seems like they are sitting around and drinking beer and watching television from what I have seen so far. It's really annoying to see people sitting around and not do a thing for this cause when they have committed forces to the cause. I'm sure most of the money we have donated to the UN is paying their salaries.

Well, since we were preparing to leave, we had some riggers come in and tie up the uparmored humvee we had. Well, there was nobody there to hook it up, and since a new SF group was with us and not supporting us, 1SG Orick and I had been tasked to hook the Hummer to the helicopter when it came in. So, the riggers told us the large bungee type cord would be hooked to the fasteners on the helicopter when it came in.

When a CH47 comes in, anything that is on the ground automatically becomes airborne as it starts to decend. So, while the chopper was coming in, it was kicking up dust, small rocks, and generally making it a living sandstorm for 1SG and myself to hook this Hummer up. The SF team sergeant and I weren't getting along too well, and so he was worthless. So, I was going to 'earn' my rigger wings the hard way. Do it without any supervision. As the chopper came in low, I could see one crew chief signaling from the bottom of the helicopter. He would be talking to the pilot while we were standing on top of the Hummer. When it started to come down, 1SG got his hooked up right away, and then the chopper started to sway a little bit, and started coming down. Well, I got on my belly and had the hook in my hand to attach, and just as I hooked it up, the chopper came very close to my body. I wasn't sure how close until I jumped down off the Hummer.

When the chopper took off with our Hummer, 1SG Orick said, you should be dead right now. The team sergeant looked at me, and said, "You had a close call there." Well, I had been so tunnel visioned on getting it hooked up; the thought of being crushed by a 22000 lb helicopter never really came across my mind. So, I said how close was it? 1SG said, "You were a few inches away from me having to tell your wife you were dead." This was the second time in 7 days I had avoided death, and I wasn't about to do it again. So I thought. . . .

1SG Orick and I put the last of our things on the ring re-supply flight on December 17. The BDE commander ordered us back on that flight, and he was firm with the order. Well, I thought since it's coming from the BDE commander in black and white (email), it must be serious. I asked no questions. We got our things, and headed out of there.

It was a little windy leaving the firebase. I was just relieved to be leaving that place. I hoped God would judge this place for the things they caused our men. I know that sounds selfish and hard-hearted, but these people that live here were bombing us, and shooting at us all the time, while smiling at us when they weren't. I was heartbroken I had to leave the men, but at the same time relieved. My anxiety I had been feeling was eased somewhat. I missed Jacob and Dale, and I knew their families had probably been notified by now. It shook my world to see them both die, and I thank God for their service. If I could go back and know to take a different route, believe me, I would have. Maybe it was freak luck that I had driven over the IED and it didn't go off. I may never know.

There is only one way to get to the firebase without destroying vehicles, and that is by helicopter. Since we were traveling by helicopter, we had total faith because they were US pilots. As we climbed up and up trying to reach the mountain range peak, I thought about relaxing back in Kandahar with a hair cut, and maybe get a hot meal. I also wanted to rest my head from all the lost sleep I was experiencing. Besides that, I had come down with something again. So, just as the helicopter was making its ascent, wind had picked up and literally pushed our helicopter a little bit. I will admit I was a little frightened. Well, as we peaked the summit of the mountain, the helicopter dropped in altitude sharply. 1SG said that he saw the ATV we had on board come a foot off the ground. One of the crew chiefs were on it too, and I'm not sure what he said into the headset to the pilots, but I wouldn't want it repeated at Christmas dinner. Lips CAN be read, trust me.

I thought for a brief moment that it was going down. I thought about the helicopter that crashed in the mountains in the far east two months before with the ballots from the election, and how everyone on board was killed. Would this be my fate? Was I leaving a quagmire of unstable people, only to be plummeted to my certain death if this thing crashed? Only God would save us. I prayed silently to myself, and as I was heading to Kandahar, I could only think of my wife, and coming home in a couple weeks to the smell of her cooking. I longed to see everyone back home and hug them all. God WOULD let me do at least that.

We did arrive safely in Kandahar after a 45 minute ride, and were feeling good about being there to meet our staff. Fortunately, there was someone there to greet us, and it was refreshing that we were being manifested to fly back to Kabul on a C130. I was happy about that too. We rested and then got something to eat.

CHAPTER 12

✦

LEADERSHIP

I decided to write a chapter on something I felt was important to me: leadership. In fact, the next 2 are devoted to a short analysis, and then ways I feel leaders can best develop their subordinates into team players and efficient role players for their men. Thousands of books have been written on the subject, and most of them claim better character, integrity, blah, blah, blah. The problem is how does a person change to fit into a leadership role? Believe me it takes changing with the times.

My all time favorite baseball player is Pete Rose. I grew up in the 1970's and 80's (mom says I need to grow up still sometimes) when baseball was truly America's pastime, so I loved baseball as much as I loved my family. Pete Rose was one of the hardest playing, selfless persons I ever saw play the game. He was always running his hardest, and diving whenever he had the chance to make a great play. I saw him get walked several times, and he would sprint to first base. You won't see that nowadays with today's ballplayers. They might have to include some clause in their contract today for it. I truly believe Pete would have played baseball for a dollar. He was that dedicated to the game. Pete was a good leader not because of all the hits, or the hard playing, but he stood out in a good way for baseball. He should be inducted into the Hall of Fame because of it.

My favorite active player is Randy Johnson. He is another person who is a leader on the field. Randy participates and gives the game a needed breath of fresh air. He doesn't stand out like 'Charley Hustle,' but he does lead whatever team he is on. His expectations of winning are high, and he settles for nothing less than the best. I admire that.

What makes a great leader? Or, a leader at all? What is it that the Army doesn't have that all successful organizations have? I think Lee Iacocca shed some good light on this in his book when he referred to a private dinner attended by Vince Lombardi:

Lombardi said, "You have to start by teaching fundamentals. A player's got to know the basics of the game and how to play his position. Next, you've got to keep him in line. That's discipline. The men have no room for prima donnas."

He continued: But there have been a lot of coaches with good ball clubs who know the fundamentals and have plenty of discipline but still don't win the game. Then you come to the third ingredient: if you're going to play together as a team, you've got to care for one another. You've got to love each other. Each player has to be thinking about the next guy and saying to himself: 'If I don't block that man, Paul is going to get his legs broken. I have to do my job well in order that he can do his.'

"The difference between mediocrity and greatness," Lombardi said that night, "is the feeling these guys have for each other. Most people call it team spirit. When the players are imbued with that special feeling, you know you've got yourself a winning team.

Then he blurted out almost self-consciously, "But Lee, what am I telling you for? You run a company. It's the same thing, whether you're running a ball club or a corporation. After all, does one man build a car all by himself?"

I put that citation from Lee Iacocca's book: *Iacocca: An Autobiography* for a reason. There are a lot of men trying to lead, and they have the head smarts for memorizing things, and there are other guys who are talented enough to make good grades in their basic courses, but they lack the heart to truly lead people. Our efficiency in the Army is broken partly because the system truly needs an overhaul. There is too much room for 'good ole' boy' syndrome to keep its head above water.

I noticed a lot of guys who were out to 'medal hunt.' Any military guy who has been to an armed conflict knows exactly what Im talking about too. I knew of a bunch of guys who were put in for certain medals that probably should have been looked at twice. Men who I KNEW were in many firefights, and had some awful things happen to them, got most of their medals downgraded. Maybe there was good reason, but it doesn't justify the fact that many guys were given them for no reason other than being in a certain position, or having a certain title. Some guys bought rugs, bought souvenirs, did a lot of joyriding, and got the same bronze star I got. Good for them, they never had bullets whizzing by their heads like Mike and I did. They rarely ever left the wire. Now, I'm not trying to say the system stinks but that the system allowed certain guys to take advantage of the awards they shouldn't have gotten. Or, some other guys should have been given.

Leadership isn't about self. Leadership is about other people. Other people will always make a leader look good. We've sold out to the system of: "You do what I say, because I said so, and I look good." The way it should be is the leader makes a good choice, coaches subordinate leaders into their roles, and the troops carry out the plan while making the subordinate leader look good. The biggest thing a leader can do is not focus on the past. We see the way yesterday's leadership handled things, and we automatically think, "Well, they failed doing it, and they taught me how to do that, so we'll do that." A good leader will not focus on the problems of yesterday though. A good leader shares a vision of what tomorrow will be like. They need to have an adjustment to their present situation, and use it to shape that vision of what things CAN be like, not what they WERE like.

One time in our mess hall at Camp Blackhorse, I saw General William Shoomaker, the Army Chief of Staff, as he visited with the troops. It was a very encouraging breath of fresh air for me. There was a separate set of tables set up in the middle of the room, all ready for the other general staff and senior leadership to sit. I could see them licking their chops for the opportunity to sit and further their political exploits when he arrived. They all had aspirations of pinning another star on their collar, or making their black oak leaf a bird. When he entered the dining room though, he walked right by the table and sat down with one of the soldiers. Much to the dismay of the upper ranking leaders, he didn't even say hello to them. I was shocked, and also relieved at the same time that he wasn't anybody's lapdog. He didn't want anyone sucking up to him either. I chuckled inside, and prayed silently that more like him would follow in his footsteps. There isn't many like him left in the Army. It made me think I want to be like him too, for many reasons.

It's true that a leader needs to have a certain amount of ego. Some leaders have too much ego. A leader needs to have a good amount of ego though, it is necessary. Many feel the financial burden of a multi-billion dollar company, and the thousands of families that need their leadership. Some are pastors of churches who bear the burden of hundreds of members who need his counsel. Others have to make decisions where they know there is a high probability of combat. As the forces of nature change seasons, and wield heavy storms, a leader also must face change, and decide where their ego is placed on the image that is about to change with them.

Our change is imminent in this atmosphere of reliance on 'systems' to guide us. Hopefully the leader will look to his or her people and not a system. A commander could have the most detailed, foolproof plan in the entire theatre of operation, but it won't get executed if he doesn't have the personnel to carry out the assignment. Time and time again we were short personnel in Mazir-e-Sharif and we all had to go out on missions with people we weren't used to working with. The main things we relied on were each other and what little communication assets were available to us.

The best part about our working with each other there was that everyone viewed each other as partners on the same team. We ranked from sergeant to major, but I can't remember one time where we used our rank to determine who would go where. I mean, there were obviously times when the officers had to complete risk assessment, but I can't remember a time when we used rank to go over each other's head. Everybody had something to contribute in each field. Being National Guardsman we had police officers, correctional officers, post office carriers, financial gurus (me), and had some guys who were in business for themselves. It was nice to have that kind of input because somebody always had something they could share.

I remember someone saying once, "The Army is like a giant ball of chaos. The trick isn't to change it into order; the trick is to manage it." I thought about that long and hard and knew that a leader must be able to ride the changes out for the better. I truly believe that adversity makes a person become better with time. Doing something rather than watching someone else do it is a lot easier and teaches much better lessons than just jumping in and expecting things to go perfectly the first time. Too many leaders are programmed by systems and therefore are poor leaders when it comes to making effective decisions when those circumstances arise.

I remember as a boy trying to hit a baseball. I saw it done on the television and how Pete Rose could get a hit almost every time. How hard could it be for a 7-year-old, right? I didn't know the mechanics involved in hitting a baseball. There are some things like watching the ball all the way to the bat, stepping into the swing, standing correctly in the batter's box, etc. The same thing goes for leaders. A person needs to practice leading and decision making in order to make the best choice for the organization. Mike and I used our 22 and 16 years of experience to help guide us, and we both came home happy that we made it.

CHAPTER 13

✪

DEVELOPING LEADERSHIP

This chapter is Don Heichel's philosophy on how to become a good leader. I have bad news for you though; it does not consist of ruling with an iron fist, or sending people to motivational seminars. What I am going to tell you works on a soldiers level, and an international level. So, here it is: leadership, Part II.

Rule One–All leaders need a mentor they can be secure in. Just like a father and a son, a baby and a mother, or a coach and a player. CPT Raqib (The first ANA commander I mentored) used to try to impress me with making a decision on his own, and he would even micromanage down to the solider level. Then out of the blue he would grab my interpreter and ask me if he made the right choice. It told me a couple things about his personality. He was unsure because he was a fairly new commander, and it also told me he needed another voice to confirm his decision. I was his mentor after all, and he respected me to give him a thumbs up.

So, the strength he had confidence in, was above him. He felt secure that he knew I could give him the advice he needed, and be safe in that choice.

Rule Two–You find a strength, and then make it stronger. A good supply sergeant, a good executive officer, a good platoon leader, whomever it is that is a strength on a person's staff needs to be made stronger. A follower will always help make a leader stronger. Encouragement or offering an expertise on something will always be a good compliment to that.

Rule Three–You must make your leader the person you want him/her to be. A person who criticizes every decision a leader makes will not be a good influence on them. All my soldiers have not agreed with all my choices, but I never made a choice that got somebody killed. My leadership almost always are counseled with and asked for input before I made a decision regarding training, schooling, or any other aspect of our operation. I take input, and then use the best pieces we have, and utilize them for the good of the cause.

Rule Four–A real leader does not rule with force. There is a word for that, and it's called tyranny. No leader that showed dictatorial traits lasted forever. No woman who was married to a man who ruled with the iron fist can say she was happy. In fact, I have found that most leaders, who are good leaders, don't really want to be a show off or in the limelight at all. They really want to be a part of something. So, by helping your leader become a leader, you really strengthen and enhance the relationship between the two of you.

Rule Five–Never rebel against the leader that you have chosen. If you want to become a better person, or make your situation better, choose to raise up your leader to lead all other leaders. You hurt yourself when you hurt your leader.

Rule Six–Never be disloyal. In *The Leadership Secrets of Colin Powell,* he says, "When we are debating an issue, loyalty means giving me your honest opinion, whether you think I'll like it or not. Disagreement, at this state, stimulates me. But, once a decision is made, the debate ends. From that point on, loyalty means executing the decision as if it were your own." Undercutting a leader or trying to play down a decision will ultimately cause dissent and mutiny amongst the ranks. If a commander is going to become good, or great, they need loyal subordinate leaders, and loyal soldiers. Nobody ever erected a statue to a critic, and they never will. If you see somebody cutting down your leaders, don't follow them!

Rule Seven–Follow the leaders, not the followers. This

is extremely important to a leader. If you stand up for your leader, walking away from the critic will say a thousand words. Sometimes it's even important to say, "Hey, maybe there is something missing they we don't know." "We don't have the same information the leaders have, maybe we should just follow, and let them lead." I wish it were that easy, but truthfully most soldiers have an instinct that is called human nature. Its nature that allows we humans to rebel and we can't stop it. Guess what?! Use your skills to say no to human nature, and you're on your way to building your character, and building your leader to where you need him/her to be!

Well, not much to sink your teeth into, but this works in all cultures, I promise. It has worked with US soldiers, and Afghani soldiers. Most leadership books I have read says you need to change this or that, not many tell you exactly 'how-to.' I hope this has given you something that you can use.

CHAPTER 14

✪

QUESTIONS

How is it going over there? What do you think about us being there? Are you glad you're home? Yes, to the last question. I get the first two questions most often now that I am home, so I'll try to give you my unabridged version of those.

As far as morale of the troops, I would say it is extremely high. Many guys are overwhelmed with care packages, cards, gifts, and attention they would not have gotten otherwise. America has truly come together when we needed. I'll try to explain what it's like there and whether or not a person would like to visit or not.

Driving in Afghanistan is a treat. There is only one paved road in the entire country, so it becomes an enigma to navigate around in trucks, humvee's and other vehicles. The terrain is simply horrible, with rocks and holes and dust. A person cannot avoid the dust. It blows and gets stirred up all the time, so sometimes when driving with night vision on, with the vehicles lights off, it is like driving through a blinding snowstorm in Wisconsin. We varied our routes all the time to keep the enemy from gathering intelligence on patterns we developed. We really didn't want to give them anymore than they needed to plant an IED on a route they knew we frequented.

Most Afghanis do not have a driver's license. It was not uncommon to see a 14- or 15-year-old kid driving a taxi for a living. We tried to steer clear of high volume of traffic when we could but on the larger ring road, we couldn't help it.

The scenery in Afghanistan is beautiful in some places,

other places it looks like the desert in Utah. We found the people living in both places were rather friendly to us, and most of the people want us there. The political entities with taliban connections though try to use propaganda to rebut that argument.

We are there to keep terrorism from making a menace of Afghanistan. For thousands of years Afghanistan was a country nobody really cared about, except the people that live there. Now a majority of the people want to feel accepted by the rest of the world. They want to belong to a cause that allows happiness to continue for everyone. The problem is that their infrastructure is totally destroyed. Through our help though, we are helping to rebuild it with a coalition effort. There are Dutch there, Italians, British, French (who sit at the airport while everyone else fights), German, Romanian, and a host of other nations helping in the rebuilding efforts. These are just a few whom I crossed paths with at one time or another.

Terror is the main way the taliban gain their momentum. They frighten people with death, and even use killing family members to coerce submission. They want everyone to basically live in the stone ages, with no electricity, no cars, nothing except total submission to their agenda. That's exactly what it is too, because the taliban use religion for the convenience of making their point. They make up things that aren't even in the Koran. Like killing people. Every single Muslim I talked to said killing people is against the Islamic belief.

I have heard of some men having 3 or 4 wives also. This also is a big problem with their religion. They want to somehow satisfy a sexual desire, and then when a woman becomes older and her appeal is lost, they use religion as a way to gain a younger wife. But, from the ones I talked to, they stated that when a man gains another spouse, the fighting inside the house starts. Of course it does! Human nature and jealousy, as well as disease and confusion are all a formula for disaster. Funny how God made one man and one woman, not one man and three women.

Well, the truth is, having Americans over there is helping their culture reach new thinking. The ones who want to speak out against using religion as a matter of convenience are starting to spring up now. I think it may be a few years before the country starts real change, and progress toward democracy, but its getting there. There are still too many warlords there that want to rule their territory how they see fit, instead of using their skills to further the development of the country as a whole. I personally think that there are warlords just waiting for President Karzai to die so they can take over for themselves.

Well, how are we doing? The US troops called to be in Afghanistan are using this time to help with the government transition to order and not disorder. It is becoming more of a containment now that there is a form of government in place. Hopefully the local police officials won't be bought by corruption and greed, and they will continue with the mission once we leave. I think a NATO effort can be good for the cause, and I hope more countries will step up with funding for helping the rebuilding effort.

The main problem facing our troops there is that there is still radical Al Qaeda cells operating in Afghanistan, and we need some help from informants to root out these minor problems. I have no doubt there will be a ceasing of Al Qaeda's activities one day. We are seeing a number of taliban leaders give up their radical activities, and that's encouraging. The northern part of Afghanistan doesn't have many problems right now, because it's a little more independent and educated than the population in the south. That's been part of the problem for years. The taliban kept people uneducated, and therefore created a scenario where people are afraid to think for themselves. It won't take much for the people to stand up and use their own intuition to take it back, because the taliban is hanging by a thread at this point.

CHAPTER 15

✪

THANKS

I hope you enjoyed my sharing a little bit of the thoughts and opinions I have presented in this book. I kept most of the thoughts I had in a journal and through letters to my wife. I wanted to take time to tell a few people thank you for the gifts and cards, and care packages I received while I was over in Afghanistan. Most of the stuffed animals were handed out personally by myself, but on one occasion, I needed help from a fellow soldier, there was simply too many to hand out.

Anyway, thank you to Tess, my wife. She wrote almost everyday, cut out newspaper articles, made me some little things to keep by my side, and prayed for me everyday. For that, she saved my life. I literally received hundreds of letters from her. Most people don't know it, but in the 4 years we've been married, we have spent 2.5 of that apart from each other. It was difficult for both of us, but I believe it has made us stronger.

THANK YOU FOR THE CARE PACKAGES AND LETTERS:

Wayne & Janice Dingman

Al Woolum

Joan & Adrian Lauer

Mrs. Estep's 2nd grade class: Tim, Eric, Destiny, Abby, Elizabeth, Xavier, Allen, Justin, Gabe, Sarah, and the others who didn't sign their names. ☺

Darold & Connie Willis (especially for the largest bottle of shampoo I have ever seen)

Mr. & Mrs. Edward Gruss

Mr. & Mrs. Wayne Graffis

Mr. & Mrs. Jim Kaufman Sr. (and the Sat. Night Bowling League)

Tom & Sandie Hill

Mr. & Mrs. Charles Tyskie

Dottie Johnson

Jim & Norlyn Stahnke

Pauline and Jeanne Callen

Linda Mager

Kelli Van Ness

Nancy Geary and the Foresters

Mr. & Mrs. Ed Kuta

Mr. & Mrs. Larry Burchiel

A little girl from Evernon Jr. High School named Jazmine

Mr. & Mrs. Greg Kelver

Mrs. Pam Frink

John Henriott and MOMS, American Legion Post 83

Norma Zeimet

Mr. & Mrs. Dwaine Koch (Spongedaddy.com)

Mrs. "M" from American Legion Post 83

Girl Scouts Troop 248

Mr. & Mrs. Don Heichel Sr.

Mr. & Mrs. Al Parsons

Natasha Gordon for the inspiring letters

Mark Rutherford and the Libertarian Party of Indiana and Laporte County

Mr. Jeff Williams

Ernie Simmons (Estorm)

Mr. & Mrs. David Jarvis

Gary Zweinski

The Late Dan Ottman

The Professional Bowlers Association

Michiana Bowlers Association for the thoughts and prayers (Thanks Chris!!)

Jerry Scrivnor and the Vietnam Veterans of Laporte County

The Wall Gang

Mr. & Mrs. Cary Kirkham

Mr. & Mrs. Jeff Sellers

Many others who have prayed, and sent things that I cannot find the address to.

I tried to include everyone, and if I missed somebody specifically, please accept my apology. The postal system lost one of my boxes I sent home, and unfortunately, some of the addresses and names I had were in there.

I especially thank George Heichel, my grandfather who spent four years in the South Pacific during World War II, stopping the terror of the Japanese, defending freedom, and bringing democracy to the islands in his area. His service means more to me than words can say. Our World War II veterans deserve the greatest thank you.

I pray everyone overseas, defending our nation and bringing democracy to Iraq and Afghanistan come home safely. If my wife and kids didn't need me so much, I would still be there. I will continue to support our troops, and especially the leaders who must make difficult decisions. Your level-headedness will ensure the safety of your men, and also bring a good reflection upon our great nation. We are proud of all of you, and will pray for you . . .

ACRONYMN APPENDIX

ANA-Afghan National Army

AO-Area of Operation

ARCOM-Army Commendation

AT-Annual Training

ATV-All Terrain Vehicle

BDE-Brigade

BDU-Battle Dress Uniform

BN - Battalion

BSM-Bronze Star Medal (A REAL BSM has a "V" device on it)

CIA-Central Intelligence Agency

CIB-Combat Infantryman Badge

CLS-Combat Life Saver

COL - Colonel

CPT-Captain

DR-Deh Rawood

ETT-Embedded Training Team

FB - Firebase

FBI-Federal Bureau of Investigation

FRG-Family Readiness Group

GMV-Like a HMMWV, except much deadlier

GPS–Global Positioning System

HMMWV–High Mobility Multipurpose Wheeled Vehicle

ID–Identification, or Infantry Division

IED–Improvised Explosive Device

IR–Infrared

LMTV–Call it a troop carrier

LTC–Lieutenant Colonel

MEDEVAC–Medical Evacuation

MRE–Meal Ready to Eat

NATO–See UN

NCO–Non-commissioned Officer

OCS–Officer Candidate School

OPCON–Operational Control

PUC–Person under control

QRF–Quick Response Force

RIP–Relief in Place

ROE–Rules of Engagement

RPG–Rocket Propelled Grenade

SECFOR–Security Force

SF–Special Forces

TK–Tarin Kowt

TTP–Tactical Training Point

UBL–Uniform Basic Load

UN–Like NATO, except totally worthless

US–United States

1SG–First Sergeant

PICTURES

August 2006: Welcome home party coordinated by my wife: Tess.

December 2004: When I was due to fly from Kandahar to Bagram, Santa hired me to be an elf for an hour or so.

October 2004: Afghani soliders working on a plan to
fix the flat tire(s) we had on this troop carrier.

In Mazir-E-Sharif with my second interpreter, Aimal.

Mike and I coordinated mortar training with a US mortrar platoon and our Afghani soliders for the day.

The Taliban destroyed several delivery trucks on this mountain pass. We found 2 IED's coming back to this truck, luckily they were blown up by the SE engineer.

Preparing for a mission inside our firebase.

A look at Deh Ranood from firebase Tycz.

It's estimated that Afghanistan has over 6 million mines buried in it.

Receiving the combat infantryman's badge. The BDE CDR agreed to pin on the one my grandfather received 60 years ago in the South Pacific.

2 Afghani soldiers learn how to account their weapons.

An IED that wounded 2 personnels after a routine mission.

On a mission with 2 soldiers from a British unit.

Mike and I waiting for a ride to Deh Rawood at the Kandahar airfield.

My dad: Don Heichel Sr., daughter: Sarah Heichel,
and nephew: Andrew Hill welcoming me back home in
Indianapolis, shortly after I landed, Home Sweet Home.

Contact author Donald Heichel
or order more copies of this book at

TATE PUBLISHING, LLC

127 East Trade Center Terrace
Mustang, Oklahoma 73064

(888) 361 - 9473

Tate Publishing, LLC

www.tatepublishing.com